What KIDS Need to SUCCEED

Proven, Practical Ways to Raise Good Kids

Revised & Updated 3rd Edition

Peter L. Benson, Ph.D., Judy Galbraith, M.A.,
and Pamela Espeland

Library of Congress Cataloging-in-Publication Data
Benson, Peter L.
  What kids need to succeed : proven, practical ways to raise good kids /
Peter L. Benson, Judy Galbraith, and Pamela Espeland. — Rev. & updated 3rd ed.
      p. cm.
  Includes index.
  ISBN 978-1-57542-397-5
  1. Child rearing—United States. 2. Parenting—United States. 3. Self-esteem in children—United States. I. Galbraith, Judy. II. Espeland, Pamela, 1951– III. Title.
  HQ769.B5118 2011
  649'.100973—dc23   2012002188

eBook ISBN: 978-1-57542-661-7

The 40 Developmental Assets information contained in this publication is used with permission and is based on Search Institute's copyrighted and trademarked intellectual property. Copyright © 1997, 2006 Search Institute. No other use is permitted without prior permission from Search Institute, 615 First Avenue NE, Minneapolis, MN 55413; 800-888-7828; www.search-institute.org. All rights reserved.

Cover and interior design by Michelle Lee
Cover photo © Image Source/Jupiterimages;
photo page 29 © Godfer/Dreamstime.com;
photo page 131 © istockphoto.com/ranplett

10 9 8 7 6 5 4 3 2 1
Printed in the United States of America

**Printed on
recycled paper**

including 50%
post-consumer waste

Free Spirit Publishing Inc.
Minneapolis, MN
(612) 338-2068
help4kids@freespirit.com
www.freespirit.com

Free Spirit Publishing is a member of the Green Press Initiative, and we're committed to printing our books on recycled paper containing a minimum of 30% post-consumer waste (PCW). For every ton of books printed on 30% PCW recycled paper, we save 5.1 trees, 2,100 gallons of water, 114 gallons of oil, 18 pounds of air pollution, 1,230 kilowatt hours of energy, and .9 cubic yards of landfill space. At Free Spirit it's our goal to nurture not only young people, but nature too!

Contents

Foreword

Eugene C. Roehlkepartain

The ideas in this book are both simple and profound. They began modestly, growing out of a hunch that building "good stuff" in the lives of kids was as important as—or more important than—preventing the "bad stuff." Twenty years later, that idea is a massive research effort and a global movement committed to helping all kids succeed in life.

The visionary behind this idea was Peter Benson, my mentor, colleague, and friend for almost 25 years. Sadly, Peter passed away October 2, 2011. This new and updated edition of *What Kids Need to Succeed* is dedicated to his memory and to continuing his legacy of helping young people be happy, healthy, and successful.

Bringing Research and Action Together

The first edition of *What Kids Need to Succeed* began as a collaboration between Search Institute and Free Spirit Publishing in the early 1990s. Peter brought his new research on Developmental Assets and ideas about how they could be built. (As you'll read in this book, the Developmental Assets make up a research-based framework for understanding what kids need to succeed.) Our Free Spirit colleagues, Judy Galbraith and Pamela Espeland, brought their knowledge and gifts for communicating the practical wisdom of asset building to parents, teachers, and caring adults everywhere.

It was a perfect match, and the book has helped thousands of people put asset building into action.

Since those early years, Search Institute has studied assets with more than 3 million young people across North America and in countries around the world. This third edition of *What Kids Need to Succeed* incorporates data gathered in our most recent survey, which was taken by about 89,000 kids and teens around the United States. But the research is only one part of the story. Equally significant are all the people who have been transformed through their own asset-building efforts. Here's just a handful of their stories:

▸ Thousands of parents in San Jose, California, gather regularly in each other's homes for mutual support and to learn about asset-based parenting. They express their hopes and fears for their children while also reflecting on the way they grew up themselves. They discuss how they support their kids, set and enforce boundaries, teach values, and more. "It's giving them the confidence to do the little things that really make a difference," the program coordinator says.

▸ Inspired and guided by the Developmental Assets, a YMCA in Colorado began offering all sixth graders a free one-year membership so they could participate in a safe, asset-based program to help ease the transition into middle school and "learn, develop, and enhance lifelong skills" from peers and adult role models.

▸ The Royal Canadian Mounted Police began using an asset-based approach to connect with kids when they do the right thing rather than only when they make mistakes.

▸ School leaders from California to Maine are using asset building to close the achievement gap and increase student success. They give students leadership roles in school, strengthen teacher-student relationships, and create a climate in the school where all are safe and all can learn.

▸ Through asset-based empowerment programs, impoverished girls in Bangladesh have found their voices and discovered new opportunities.

▸ The Developmental Assets inspired young people in Oklahoma to research, create, and share a media literacy education program that empowers kids and teens to take control of media in their lives and encourages them to ask questions before believing what advertisers tell them.

> **Once these ideas get into your head and heart, they stick with you. You think differently about where you live and how you spend your time. This book gets inside you and transforms you.**

▸ A boys' school in Toronto, Canada, uses the Developmental Assets to help young men become more engaged in school and to create a healthy climate throughout the school. The approach has been so successful that representatives of other schools have visited to learn what they're doing.

▸ Using the assets as a foundation, the city of Hampton, Virginia, hired young people to be city planners, helping other city staff and elected leaders do research and make critical recommendations about how to make their city a great place to grow up. Similarly, Middletown, Connecticut, added young people to 12 city boards and commissions after the mayor learned that only 19 percent of Middletown kids and teens felt that their community valued them.

Despite many changes in technology, politics, science, and popular culture, the asset-building approach remains relevant and strong more than two decades after it was introduced. What has been "sticky" about this idea?

The inspiring examples go on and on. That's the good news: Great people are working together to help kids succeed. The challenge is that we still have a long way to go. Too few young people have a strong enough base of Developmental Assets. Study after study (including the data in this book) shows that *young people have, on average, only about half of the assets.* We can—we *must*—do better. That requires each of us to find our own ways to build assets with and for the young people in our lives. This book will give you the ideas and inspiration you need to do just that.

More Than 20 Years of Success

A lot of ideas don't stick around for 20-plus years. In 1990, the year the assets were released, the first Saturn cars came to market. Margaret Thatcher resigned from her post as British prime minister, and East Germany and West Germany became one country. The first Gulf War hadn't started. The term "World Wide Web" was coined that year, but most of us hadn't heard of email or the Internet yet. Jon Bon Jovi, Billy Joel, and Garth Brooks ruled the radio airwaves, and many of us were listening to cassette tapes on the Sony Walkman. And yet, despite many changes in technology, politics, science, and popular culture, the asset-building approach remains relevant and strong more than two decades after it was introduced. What has been "sticky" about this idea?

I can offer my personal answer to that question, based on my own experience as a parent. My oldest son was born the same year Search Institute released the Developmental Assets. So my wife and I adopted the assets as a guide for the choices we made as parents and as a family. And the assets have continued to help us every year—and, in fact, every day—that we've been parents. Once these ideas get into your head and heart, they stick with you. You begin to think differently about parenting. You think differently about where you live and how you spend your time. You listen to and walk beside your child differently. You don't just buy this book, read it, and put it on the shelf. This book gets inside you and transforms you.

At least, that's what has happened for me. I hope you experience the same transformation, whether you're a parent, a teacher, a youth worker, a neighbor, a grandparent, or someone else dedicated to kids. Each of us has a part to play in the mission shared by Peter Benson, Search Institute, and Free Spirit Publishing: making the world a better place for kids—one person, family, and community at a time.

Eugene C. Roehlkepartain
Acting President & CEO
Search Institute, Minneapolis, MN

Introduction

What Do Kids Really Need?

Since the first edition of *What Kids Need to Succeed* was published nearly two decades ago, many things have changed.

In particular, at that time few of us could have imagined the degree to which the Internet would one day permeate our lives—and the lives of our kids. We had never heard of Facebook or Twitter, and we were strangers to the idea of Googling. And many of us never guessed that so many kids would spend so much of their time tapping away at smartphones and laptops, which—with all their benefits— also bring new concerns and their own unique set of drawbacks.

But even in this rapidly changing world, one thing remains constant: our concern for our young people. We're concerned about our own kids, our neighbors' kids, the students in our classrooms, the children in our faith communities, and kids in general. All of us have read stories and heard alarming facts about bullying, school failure, substance abuse, violence, sexually transmitted diseases, teen pregnancy, eating disorders, and suicide. While watching the news, we've seen images of troubled, alienated, and angry kids who seem unreachable. And we often feel powerless to help. It seems as though no program, initiative, strategy, or organization is working long enough, hard enough, or for enough kids.

1

All of this can feel overwhelming. It can be depressing, frustrating, and frightening.

But here's the good news: *It doesn't have to be this way.*

What if you knew specific, practical things you could do to make a tremendous difference in young people's lives? And what if you saw proof that these specific, practical things really work?

The title of this book, *What Kids Need to Succeed,* is not an exaggeration. It's a simple statement of what you'll find here: powerful ideas for positive change. If you're willing to try these ideas, they can ensure a better future for the young people you know personally, for all young people in your community, and—ultimately—for everyone.

So, what *do* kids need to succeed? This, too, may seem surprisingly simple: *What kids really need are adults who care.*

It All Began with a Series of Surveys

More than two decades of research and data support the ideas in this book. From September 1989 through March 1990, students in grades six through twelve were given a 152-item inventory called "Profiles of Student Life: Attitudes and Behaviors." The inventory was developed by Search Institute, a nonprofit organization based in Minneapolis, Minnesota, that specializes in research on children and teens. It was sponsored by RespecTeen, a national program of Lutheran Brotherhood, a nonprofit corporation that provides financial services and community service opportunities for Lutherans.

More than 46,000 students in 111 communities and 25 states took part in the initial survey. The results were published in 1990 by Lutheran Brotherhood and in 1993 by Search Institute as *The Troubled Journey: A Portrait of 6th–12th Grade Youth.*

Meanwhile, the use of the survey continued and grew. Eventually more than 250,000 young people in 600 communities and 33 states—in small towns, suburbs, and big cities; in two-parent, single-parent, and adoptive families; in poverty, the middle class, and affluence—took the original Search Institute inventory. The first edition of *What Kids Need to Succeed*, published in 1994, was based on the results of that survey.

> **So, what *do* kids need to succeed? What kids really need are adults who care.**

In 1996, the survey was revised and expanded to gather even more information about kids' lives. Each year, more and more communities wanted to learn about what their kids needed to succeed. Today, more than 3 million young people in thousands of communities across the United States—as well as in other countries—have been surveyed. The facts and figures in this revised and updated third edition of *What Kids Need to Succeed* are based on surveys conducted in 2010. In all, this latest data includes survey results from 89,000 young people in 26 states.

The Surveys Revealed Amazing Things

When Search Institute analyzed the results of those first surveys more than two decades ago, we asked ourselves: Why do some kids grow up with ease, while others struggle? Why do some kids get involved in dangerous activities, while others spend their time contributing to society? Why do some kids "beat the odds" in difficult situations, while others seem to be trapped by their circumstances? We recognized that many factors influence why some young people succeed in life and others have a harder time—including financial resources, genetics, and trauma. These factors can be difficult or even impossible to change, *but they aren't all that matter.* Our surveys revealed that a significant factor in the difference between troubled kids and those leading healthy, productive lives is the presence (or absence) of what we decided to call **Developmental Assets.**

The usual definition of *assets* is "property or resources." We chose this term because the things we identified—which are essentially building blocks for human development—act like assets in a young person's life. They increase in value over time. They provide a sense of security. They are resources upon which a child or teen can draw again and again. They help young people make wise decisions, choose positive paths, and grow up competent, caring, and responsible. And they're cumulative, meaning that *the more assets a young person has, the better.*

We first identified 30 Developmental Assets, and later expanded the list to 40. These assets are good things that every young person needs in his or her life. The first 20 are **external assets.** These are things in a young person's environment (home, school, and community) that support, nurture, and empower him or her, set boundaries and expectations, and help him or her make constructive use of time. The external assets are:

Support

1. Family Support
2. Positive Family Communication
3. Other Adult Relationships
4. Caring Neighborhood
5. Caring School Climate
6. Parent Involvement in Schooling

Empowerment

7. Community Values Youth
8. Youth as Resources
9. Service to Others
10. Safety

Boundaries and Expectations

11. Family Boundaries
12. School Boundaries
13. Neighborhood Boundaries
14. Adult Role Models
15. Positive Peer Influence
16. High Expectations

Constructive Use of Time

17. Creative Activities
18. Youth Programs
19. Religious Community
20. Time at Home

The next 20 are **internal assets**—attitudes, values, and competencies that belong in the head and heart of every child. The internal assets are:

Commitment to Learning

21. Achievement Motivation
22. School Engagement
23. Homework
24. Bonding to School
25. Reading for Pleasure

Positive Values

26. Caring
27. Equality and Social Justice
28. Integrity
29. Honesty
30. Responsibility
31. Restraint

Social Competencies

32. Planning and Decision Making
33. Interpersonal Competence
34. Cultural Competence
35. Resistance Skills
36. Peaceful Conflict Resolution

Positive Identity

37. Personal Power

38. Self-Esteem

39. Sense of Purpose

40. Positive View of Personal Future

How many of these Developmental Assets do kids in the United States have today? Although they should have at least 31, most have only 20—a start, but not nearly enough. Here's a graph of what we found:

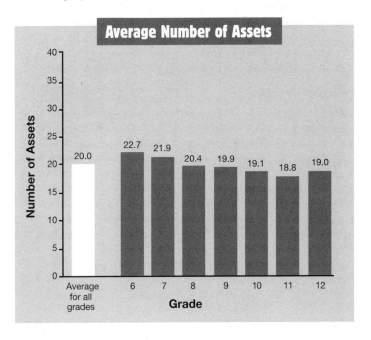

Average Number of Assets

Number of Assets:
- Average for all grades: 20.0
- Grade 6: 22.7
- Grade 7: 21.9
- Grade 8: 20.4
- Grade 9: 19.9
- Grade 10: 19.1
- Grade 11: 18.8
- Grade 12: 19.0

We also learned that the number of assets kids have seems to decline as kids age. In general, older teens have fewer assets than younger kids do. And boys generally have fewer assets (18.8) than girls (21.3).

Here's another way of looking at how many assets young people have, across genders and grades:

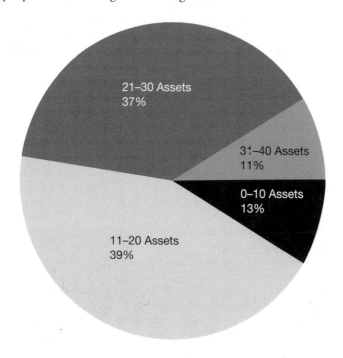

More Assets Mean Fewer Problem Behaviors

We know that the assets have a clear, real-world impact on kids' lives. But how do we know that the total number of assets makes a difference? When we looked for specific high-risk behaviors—behaviors that are known to potentially limit psychological, physical, or economic well-being during adolescence or adulthood—our survey revealed how powerful the assets really are. *Young people who have more assets are much less likely to get involved in these problem behaviors.* See for yourself:

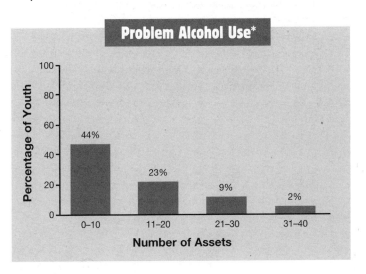

*Has used alcohol three or more times in the past 30 days or gotten drunk once or more in the past two weeks

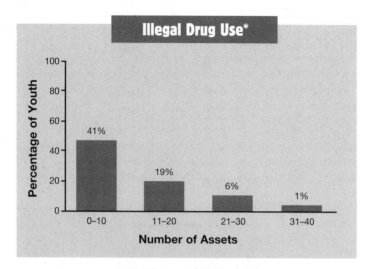

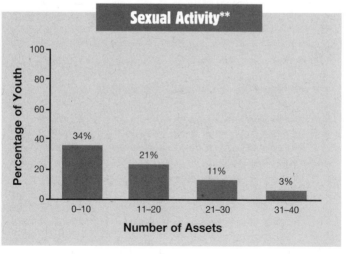

*Used illegal drugs multiple times in the past 12 months
**Has had sexual intercourse three or more times in lifetime

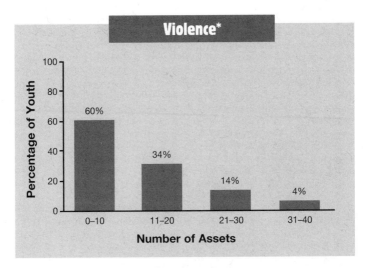

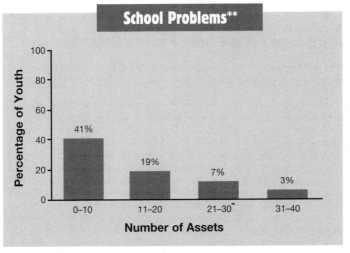

*Has engaged in three or more acts of fighting, hitting, injuring a person, carrying or using a weapon, or threatening physical harm in the past 12 months
**Has skipped school two or more days in the last four weeks and/or has below a C average

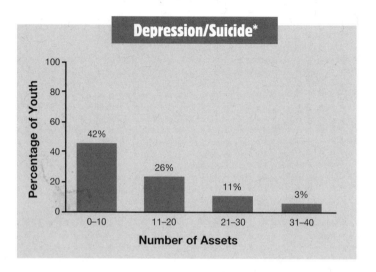

More Assets Mean More Positive Behaviors

We also found that the Developmental Assets work the other way, too. Young people who have more assets are much *more* likely to get involved in positive, thriving behaviors. Take a look at the evidence in the graphs that follow:

*Is frequently depressed and/or has attempted suicide

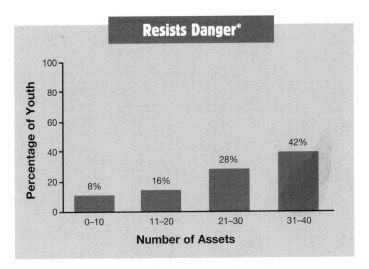

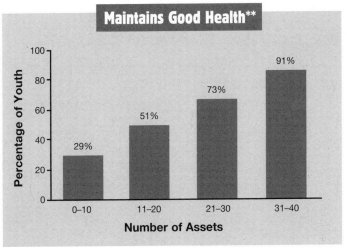

*Avoids doing things that are dangerous
**Pays attention to healthy nutrition and exercise

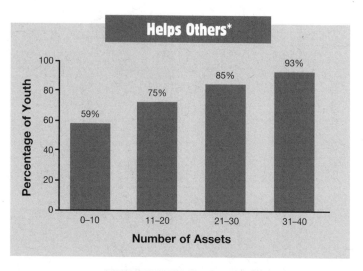

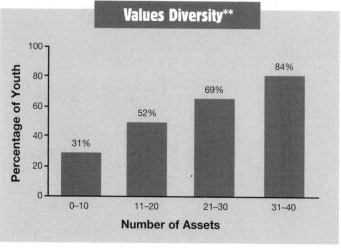

*Helps friends or neighbors one or more hours per week
**Places high importance on getting to know people of other racial/ethnic groups

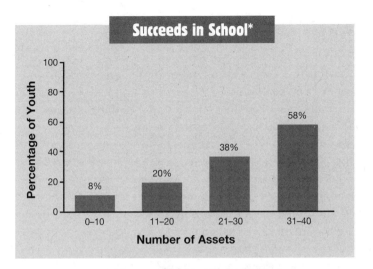

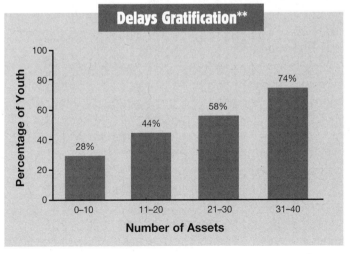

*Gets mostly A's on report card
**Saves money for something special rather than spending it all right away

You Can Be an Asset Builder

What Kids Need to Succeed describes the assets and gives you concrete, practical suggestions for building them in young people. As you can see from the list on pages 5–7, the assets aren't complicated. Most cost nothing in terms of money. Many are things you may already be doing. You won't find any radical, experimental, or theoretical ideas in this book. What you will find is a commonsense approach to raising good kids so they're free to grow into competent, contributing, responsible, compassionate adults.

In reality, there are probably dozens of other assets that are also important to helping young people succeed, but this list is a great place to get started. If our kids could have many of these assets, all of us would be better off. As you start thinking seriously about asset building, you'll likely find many other ways to provide positive support for the young people in your life.

Not every idea you'll read about here will work for everyone. If you try an idea with a particular child or group and it doesn't work, don't get discouraged, and don't stop there. Keep reading! We've included *more than 900 ideas* for families, schools, communities, and faith communities. You're sure to find one that gets results . . . and then you'll find another, and another, and another.

Something to note: This book does not attempt to describe everything you need to know or do before implementing an idea. For example, if we suggest that you recruit adult volunteers into a school, community organization, or faith community, you'll need to ensure that appropriate systems are in place to provide a safe, enriching environment for everyone, both kids *and* adults.

Despite the best efforts of concerned and involved adults, not every young person will end up with all 40 assets firmly in place. But it's important to remember that *the more assets a young person has, the better.* This is not wishful thinking. It's a fact that is clearly supported by the survey results.

You Can Start Today

Whether you're a parent, a teacher, a community or religious leader, or just an adult who wants to help kids, you can begin building assets today. This positive approach to youth development is not about crisis management, although young people who have these assets face fewer crises. It is not about stopping and preventing problems, although young people who have these assets face (and create) fewer problems. Instead, it's about investing wisely in our young people, increasing their exposure to positive, constructive activities, and instilling in them values and skills that will guide them from the inside.

The ideas behind the Developmental Assets are not complicated. But this doesn't mean that building the assets is always simple, or that doing so is a quick fix. Asset building takes time and commitment from caring adults, both individually and in community. It's worth it *because it works.*

This book presents literally hundreds of practical ideas for parents, schools, communities, and faith communities to try. We have kept them brief and to the point, because we mean this to be an action handbook, not a lengthy dissertation. You won't find step-by-step instructions or

A WORD ABOUT THE WORDS WE USE

We use the words *parents* and *parent* throughout this book to indicate children's primary caregivers. Of course, not all kids live with two biological parents or even one biological parent. Rather than spell out "biological parent, adoptive parent, step-parent, foster parent, grandparent, guardian, or whatever" each time we refer to a primary caregiver, we've opted for simplicity and brevity. If you're an adult who's raising and guiding a child, then when we say "parent," we mean you.

We use the term *faith community* to indicate the people with whom you worship, and *place of worship* to indicate where you go. We have chosen these terms over "congregation," "church," "temple," "synagogue," "mosque," "meeting house," and others that refer to specific faiths because we want to be sure to communicate the importance of asset building in *all* faith communities and traditions.

This book has been written for a broad, general audience. As you share the information and discuss the assets with others, we hope you will use the words that feel most comfortable to you.

how-tos. You'll need to decide how to shape the ideas to suit your particular circumstances. Asset building is most effective and most successful when you tailor it to your community and the needs of its young people. So before you dive in, ask yourself—and your fellow asset builders—some key questions. What resources are available to you? What programs and activities already exist? What other adults can help you? Get input from young people, too. What do they want and need? And how can they help?

In our experience, when people first learn about the assets and their power to change lives, they want to get started right away. Use this book as a jumping-off point. Get together with your family, friends, and neighbors to plan ways to try these ideas in your community. Brainstorm your own ideas.

Throughout this book, you'll also find special sections called "Tips for Teens: Build Your Own Assets." Share these with the young people you know. You may want to start by telling them about the study and showing them the charts on pages 9–15. Most kids really *want* to stay out of trouble and succeed in life. When they understand how powerful the assets can be, they may feel motivated and decide to get involved in shaping their own futures.

Here are six key points to keep in mind along the way:

1. **Everyone can build assets.** All adults, teens, and children can play a role. Building assets requires consistent messages across a community.

2. **All young people need assets.** While it's crucial to pay special attention to those young people who have the least (economically or emotionally), *all* young people can benefit from adding more assets and developing the assets they already have.

3. **Relationships are critical**. Strong relationships among adults and young people, young people and their peers, and teenagers and children are central to asset building.

4. **Asset building is an ongoing process.** It starts when a child is born, and it continues through high school—and beyond.

5. **Consistent messages are important.** Young people need to receive consistent messages from their families, schools, communities, and other sources about what's important and what's expected.

6. **Intentional redundancy is important.** Assets must be continually reinforced across the years and in all areas of a young person's life.

Your Turn

We'd love to hear your success stories, and we welcome your suggestions for building assets in young people. Let us know how these ideas work for you and share your own experiences and new ideas by emailing us at help4kids@freespirit.com, or by writing to us at this address:

Free Spirit Publishing Inc.
217 Fifth Avenue North, Suite 200
Minneapolis, MN 55401-1299

Caring adults and committed communities have been building assets across the nation and the world for close to two decades, ever since the first edition of *What Kids Need to Succeed* was published. It's our great hope that asset building will continue to take place around the globe, and that people in every community will keep striving to create a better, more positive future for all children.

So let's get to work.

Add Up Your Assets
Checklists for Kids and Parents

The average young person we surveyed has 20 assets out of the 40 we identified. If you're a parent, you're probably wondering how many assets your child already has. The checklists that follow can help you find out.

The checklist on pages 23–25 is for kids and teens themselves; the one on pages 26–28 is for parents. Both are adaptations of the original Search Institute youth surveys.* You can find free downloads of the checklists at www.freespirit.com/success.

1. **Start by making printouts or photocopies of each checklist.** You may have more than one child, and you may want to return to the checklists later, after trying some of the suggestions in this book, so we recommend that you not write in the book itself.

2. **Complete the checklists separately.** Have each person total her or his responses.

3. **Afterward, meet with your child to share and discuss your responses and perceptions.** Does your child report more or fewer assets than you expected? Do you and your child have different ideas about the assets that are present in your child's life? You may be surprised by something your child says. If so, try extending the conversation by saying something like, "I didn't know

*Please note that these checklists are not intended nor appropriate as scientific or accurate measurements of the Developmental Assets. They are provided here to give you a starting point for discussion and awareness.

that! Tell me more. . . ." As you'll see, the checklists provide great opportunities for conversation and discovery.

Parents and kids who have talked about the checklists have found this to be an enriching experience in and of itself. It's also an asset builder. When you take the time to talk seriously about the checklists, you're strengthening Asset #2: Positive Family Communication.

On each checklist, the numbers of the statements correspond to the numbers assigned to the assets. You may want to identify the assets that seem to be missing from your child's life and then turn directly to the pages in this book that describe ways to build those assets.

A Checklist for Kids and Teens

Check each statement that is true for you.

☐ **1.** I feel loved and supported in my family.

☐ **2.** I can go to my parents or guardians for advice and support. I have frequent, in-depth conversations with them.

☐ **3.** I know three or more other adults (besides my parents or guardians) who I can go to for advice and support.

☐ **4.** My neighbors encourage and support me.

☐ **5.** My school provides a caring, encouraging environment.

☐ **6.** My parents or guardians help me succeed in school.

☐ **7.** I feel valued by adults in my community.

☐ **8.** I am given useful roles in my community.

☐ **9.** I serve in my community one hour or more each week.

☐ **10.** I feel safe at home, at school, and in my neighborhood.

☐ **11.** My family has clear rules and consequences for my behavior, and they monitor my whereabouts.

☐ **12.** My school has clear rules and consequences for behavior.

☐ **13.** Neighbors take responsibility for monitoring my behavior.

☐ **14.** My parents or guardians and other adults in my life model positive, responsible behavior.

☐ **15.** My best friends model responsible behavior.

☐ **16.** My parents or guardians and my teachers encourage me to do well.

☐ **17.** I spend three or more hours each week in lessons or practice in music, theater, or other arts.

☐ **18.** I spend three or more hours each week in school or community sports, clubs, or organizations.

☐ **19.** I spend one hour or more each week in religious services or participating in a faith community.

☐ **20.** I go out with friends "with nothing special to do" two or fewer nights each week.

☐ **21.** I want to do well in school.

☐ **22.** I like to learn new things.

☐ **23.** I do an hour or more of homework each school day.

☐ **24.** I care about my school.

☐ **25.** I read for pleasure three or more hours each week.

☐ **26.** I believe that it's really important to help other people.

☐ **27.** I want to help promote equality and reduce world poverty and hunger.

☐ **28.** I act on my convictions. I stand up for my beliefs.

☐ **29.** I tell the truth—even when it's not easy.

- [ ] **30.** I accept and take personal responsibility for my actions and decisions.
- [ ] **31.** I believe that it's important not to be sexually active or to use alcohol or other drugs.
- [ ] **32.** I'm good at planning ahead and making decisions.
- [ ] **33.** I'm good at making and keeping friends.
- [ ] **34.** I know and am comfortable with people of different cultural, racial, and/or ethnic backgrounds.
- [ ] **35.** I resist negative peer pressure and avoid dangerous situations.
- [ ] **36.** I try to resolve conflicts nonviolently.
- [ ] **37.** I believe that I have control over many things that happen to me.
- [ ] **38.** I feel good about myself.
- [ ] **39.** I believe that my life has a purpose.
- [ ] **40.** I'm optimistic about my future.

A Checklist for Parents

Check each statement that is true for you or your child.

☐ **1.** I give my child a lot of love and support.

☐ **2.** My child can come to me for advice and support. We have frequent, in-depth conversations.

☐ **3.** My child knows three or more other adults whom he or she can go to for advice and support.

☐ **4.** Our neighbors encourage and support my child.

☐ **5.** My child's school provides a caring, encouraging environment.

☐ **6.** I'm actively involved in helping my child succeed in school.

☐ **7.** My child feels valued by adults in our community.

☐ **8.** My child is given useful roles in our community.

☐ **9.** My child serves in our community one hour or more each week.

☐ **10.** My child feels safe at home, at school, and in our neighborhood.

☐ **11.** Our family has clear rules and consequences for behavior. We monitor each other's whereabouts.

☐ **12.** My child's school has clear rules and consequences for behavior.

☐ **13.** Our neighbors take responsibility for monitoring my child's behavior.

☐ **14.** I model positive, responsible behavior, and so do other adults that my child knows.

☐ **15.** My child's best friends model responsible behavior.

☐ **16.** I encourage my child to do well, and so do my child's teachers.

☐ **17.** My child spends three or more hours each week in lessons or practice in music, theater, or other arts.

☐ **18.** My child spends three or more hours each week in school or community sports, clubs, or organizations.

☐ **19.** My child spends one hour or more each week in religious services or participating in a faith community.

☐ **20.** My child spends two or fewer nights each week out with friends "with nothing special to do."

☐ **21.** My child wants to do well in school.

☐ **22.** My child likes to learn new things.

☐ **23.** My child does an hour or more of homework each school day.

☐ **24.** My child cares about her or his school.

☐ **25.** My child reads for pleasure three or more hours each week.

☐ **26.** My child believes that it's really important to help other people.

☐ **27.** My child wants to help promote equality and reduce world poverty and hunger.

☐ **28.** My child acts on his or her convictions. My child stands up for his or her beliefs.

☐ **29.** My child tells the truth—even when it's not easy.

☐ **30.** My child accepts and takes personal responsibility for her or his actions and decisions.

☐ **31.** My child believes that it's important not to be sexually active or to use alcohol or other drugs.

☐ **32.** My child is good at planning ahead and making decisions.

☐ **33.** My child is good at making and keeping friends.

☐ **34.** My child knows and is comfortable with people of different cultural, racial, and/or ethnic backgrounds.

☐ **35.** My child resists negative peer pressure and avoids dangerous situations.

☐ **36.** My child tries to resolve conflicts nonviolently.

☐ **37.** My child believes that he or she has control over many things that happen to him or her.

☐ **38.** My child feels good about herself or himself.

☐ **39.** My child believes that his or her life has a purpose.

☐ **40.** My child is optimistic about her or his future.

BUILDING EXTERNAL ASSETS

SUPPORT

Young people need to experience care, love, and support from their families and many others. They need organizations and institutions that provide them with positive, supportive environments.

The six **support assets** are:

1. Family Support
2. Positive Family Communication
3. Other Adult Relationships
4. Caring Neighborhood
5. Caring School Climate
6. Parent Involvement in Schooling

The more love, support, and adult contacts a young person has, the more likely it is that he or she will grow up healthy.

ASSET #1
Family Support

Kids feel loved and supported in their family.

72% of the kids we surveyed have this asset in their lives.

At Home

○ Give more hugs and verbal reinforcement. Don't assume that your kids know how much you love them. Tell them.

○ Let your love for your children show in the way you look at them, the words you say, your tone of voice, and your body language.

○ It's not true that all kids want their parents to stop hugging or kissing them once they become teenagers. Ask your children to tell you what feels comfortable for them, and respect their boundaries.

○ Eat at least one meal together every day.

○ Set aside at least one evening per week for family activities. Hold a family brainstorming session to come up with a list of things you might like to do, and then agree on a few specific ideas to try. Be open to suggestions from all family members, and be willing to share your children's interests.

- If you have more than one child, encourage your kids to attend a certain number of their siblings' performances, sporting events, and other occasions.

- Spend time with each of your children individually. Try to make this a daily event—10 minutes after school, half an hour in the evening, an hour on Saturday morning. Let them know that this time you spend together is important to you.

- Talk with your kids about what would make your home more comfortable and inviting for them and their friends. Take steps to address any concerns.

- Children learn to love by example. Be loving toward yourself and your spouse or partner.

- Be your children's biggest fan.

At School

- Educate parents on how to be supportive of their children. Check with your school counselor or social worker for suggestions.

- Regularly write to or call parents to give positive messages about their child's attitude or progress, or to report on something the child did that deserves praise and recognition. Do this as often as you can—once every month, three or four times during the school year, or whatever is possible for you.

- During school conferences and parent meetings, focus on the positive.

In the Community

✪ Offer workshops for parents on positive parenting skills. Invite experts to speak on ways for parents to show love and support to their children. Allow time for parents to share their own ideas and experiences.

✪ Provide and publicize family crisis hotlines. These give family members a chance to "cool off" during a conflict. Train hotline counselors to suggest appropriate ways to respond to conflict, and to refer parents to other resources.

✪ When children call their parents—at the office, the community center, the gym, or wherever—make it a priority that parents receive the call.

In the Faith Community

✪ Sponsor family nights as a regular part of your youth programming.

✪ Sponsor celebrations of children and families.

✪ Regularly offer parent education as part of your faith community's educational programs.

✪ Make sure that your youth program isn't overplanned. Leave time for families to spend together.

ASSET #2
Positive Family Communication

Kids turn to their parents for advice and support. They have frequent, in-depth conversations with each other on a variety of topics. Parents are approachable and available when kids want to talk.

32% of the kids we surveyed have this asset in their lives.

At Home

○ Be available whenever and wherever your kids want to talk. What if you're in the middle of something? Arrange a time when you can talk—soon. *Tip:* Watch for hints. A child who hangs around usually wants to talk.

○ When your kids talk, really *listen.* Accept the fact that you won't agree on everything. Never label a child's opinions, beliefs, feelings, or experiences "silly," "stupid," "childish," or "wrong."

○ Form the habit of frequent conversation. Ask your kids *every day* about what they are doing and thinking. Tell them about your day, too.

✪ Now and then, have a family dinner during which the conversation focuses on one topic. Brainstorm as a family things you might talk about, then rotate whose turn it is to pick the topic.

✪ Spend one hour a week with each of your children individually. Whenever possible, spend a whole day together. Your kids will cherish these special times.

✪ Have a game night once a week or once a month. Board games can be a good way to get conversations started. When the focus is on some other activity, some kids feel more comfortable bringing up topics that they want to discuss with you but may feel shy about.

✪ The fewer topics you declare "off limits," the more your kids will talk to you. If you don't know the answer to a question, help your kids find it. Search the Internet, visit the library, or ask an expert together.

✪ Be willing to talk in a place that's comfortable for your child. Also, keep in mind that some kids have a hard time sitting still. Don't insist that they "settle down" before you can talk.

✪ Ask your child's opinion or advice about something important.

At School

✪ Include conversations with parents as part of homework assignments. *Example:* If you're teaching about events in the 1990s, you might assign parent interviews—"Where were you in 1995, and what were you doing?"

○ Provide parents with information about how to respond to tough questions and address sensitive issues. Check with your school counselor or social worker about handouts and brochures on bullying, drinking, drugs, HIV/AIDS, teen pregnancy, sexual behavior, suicide, and other difficult topics. Many parents want to talk with their kids about these subjects, but they don't know where to start or what to say.

○ Interact with students so they learn to interact with others.

○ Help students develop a feelings vocabulary—a variety of words they can use to express a variety of feelings. Use posters, films, literature, and online resources to explore feelings and ways to express them.

In the Community

○ Sponsor discussion nights for parents and teens. Publicize the topics in advance.

○ Teach parents how to respond appropriately when kids want to talk about difficult issues. Offer local workshops and meetings on topics of concern to your community. Invite experts to speak on ways to communicate with kids of all ages.

○ Sponsor activities and events that bring young people and parents together. Build in time for conversation.

In the Faith Community

○ Plan parent-teen events that encourage conversation, such as dinners, retreats, and discussion groups.

✪ Provide families with conversation-starter questions in the worship bulletin. Sponsor discussion groups for parents and teens.

✪ Teach communication skills to young people and adults. Include ideas and suggestions in mailings to member households.

✪ Let parents know that there is someone on staff who is available to answer their questions, offer advice, or just listen. Kids aren't the only ones who need someone to talk to.

ASSET #3
Other Adult Relationships

Kids know other adults besides their parents they can turn to for advice and support. They have frequent, in-depth conversations with them. Ideally, three or more adults play this role in their lives.

50% of the kids we surveyed have this asset in their lives.

At Home

- ✪ Give your children opportunities to spend time with other adults—trusted neighbors, favorite teachers, or relatives they feel comfortable with and enjoy being around.

- ✪ Encourage your children to join adult-sponsored groups, troops, or teams that are open to kids and/or teens.

- ✪ If your children have special interests, hobbies, or passions, arrange for them to meet adult friends of yours who share their interests.

- ✪ Take family vacations with other families.

✪ When you invite friends over for social occasions, include your children and theirs in your plans and your conversations.

✪ Get involved in your neighborhood and community. Introduce your children to people you meet.

✪ Many schools, youth organizations, and faith communities have people on staff—guidance counselors, psychologists, and others—who are specially trained to work with young people. Encourage your children to meet them and talk with them. Emphasize that talking with these people doesn't mean that your child is "troubled" or "weird." *Everyone* can benefit from talking with others about the things that worry—or inspire—them.

✪ With your child, identify the adults who regularly interact with him or her. *Examples:* teachers, coaches, club leaders, bus drivers, employers, administrators, custodians, neighbors, other family members, the parents of their friends. Write brief notes to several (or all) of them, expressing your appreciation for their care, dedication, and interest in your child.

✪ Get to know your children's friends. Welcome them into your home.

At School

✪ Have an open-door policy for students who want to talk. Be available as often as you can before and after school.

✪ Take time to ask students at least one question about themselves at every student conference or one-on-one meeting.

- Don't consider it wasted time when teachers spend time talking with students.
- Occasionally eat lunch in the cafeteria with the students.
- Be the faculty sponsor for a student club or event.
- Let parents know that there are people on staff who are willing and available to talk with kids.
- Work with parents and other adults in your community to arrange mentoring, internship, and service-learning opportunities for students.

In the Community

- Build at least one sustained, caring relationship with a child or adolescent in your community, either informally or through a local program. Talk with kids who live near you or work with you.
- Teach coaches and other adult leaders how to communicate well with teens. Encourage them to get to know the young people they interact with.
- Create opportunities for young people and adults to work and play together.
- Offer mentoring programs that match kids with caring adults. Volunteer to be a mentor.
- Sponsor career days so young people can spend time with adults who work in professions that interest them.
- Match up kids with adult volunteers for community service projects.

In the Faith Community

○ Train adult volunteers in how to talk with kids who have concerns. Publicize the fact that these volunteers are available and accessible.

○ Sponsor a mentoring program within the faith community.

○ Plan intergenerational programs and events so kids and adults can get to know each other better.

ASSET #4
Caring Neighborhood

Kids feel that their neighbors support them, encourage them, and care about them.

40% of the kids we surveyed have this asset in their lives.

At Home

✪ Introduce your children to your neighbors. If you don't know your neighbors, introduce yourself.

✪ Revive the old tradition of welcoming new neighbors with a plate of cookies or a cake.

✪ Get to know your neighbors. *Examples:* Work together on a neighborhood block party or cleanup; organize a potluck picnic or cookout; plan activities to bring adults and kids together; join or start a neighborhood group, neighborhood watch, or other club.

✪ Learn the names of every young person in your neighborhood. Smile at them and greet them by name when you see them.

✪ Show interest in your neighbors' children. When you see your neighbors, ask about their kids. Say something positive about them.

✪ Get to know five kids in your neighborhood.

✪ Recruit volunteers (senior citizens, college students, or stay-at-home parents) to wait with children at school bus stops.

✪ Encourage your children to find ways to serve in your neighborhood.

At School

✪ Invite students to identify ways they can promote caring in their neighborhoods.

✪ Assign projects that promote interaction between students and their neighbors. *Example:* Have students interview a neighbor, then report back on what they learned about her or him.

✪ Encourage students to find ways to serve in their neighborhoods. Brainstorm ideas together.

✪ Whether your school is a "neighborhood school" (drawing most of its students from the immediate area) or not, be neighborly. *Examples:* Hold an open house for people in your neighborhood; form alliances with neighborhood groups and businesses; make your auditorium available for neighborhood meetings; schedule times when your gym may be used by young people and adults from the neighborhood. If you have a computer lab, offer free or inexpensive classes for neighbors, with free public access to the Internet.

✪ Provide opportunities for young people to serve the school's neighborhood. Contact a neighborhood group to learn about activities it has planned for the future, and ask if your students can help.

✪ Encourage adults in your neighborhood to volunteer in your school. *Example:* Have senior citizens visit as "lunchtime listeners." Invite them to sit at cafeteria tables and talk with students.

In the Community

✪ Encourage your friends and neighbors to get to know the young people who live near them and to make young people a priority.

✪ Sponsor neighborhood get-togethers. *Examples:* block parties, potluck dinners, ice-cream socials, fall festivals, carnivals.

✪ Organize informal activities (such as pick-up basketball) for kids and teens in the neighborhood.

✪ Let kids in your neighborhood know that your house is a "safe house"—someplace they can go for help or extra support.

✪ Work with children and teenagers to create a neighborhood garden, playground, or park.

✪ Create a neighborhood website; start a neighborhood newsletter or newspaper; publish a neighborhood directory.

✪ Invite young people to participate in a neighborhood fund-raiser. Find out what kids wish their neighborhood had (*examples:* a place to skateboard, a community garden), or didn't have (*examples:* graffiti, litter in the streets) and vote on a project to complete with the money you raise.

✪ Support neighborhood groups. Work to strengthen neighborhood watch programs.

✪ Bring together representatives from several neighborhoods and develop plans and strategies for creating caring neighborhoods. Involve kids in some of your planning sessions and decision making.

In the Faith Community

✪ Encourage all members of the faith community to get to know young people in their neighborhoods. Emphasize the importance of caring neighborhoods for kids and teens, and provide ideas for action.

✪ Encourage children and teens to form relationships with their neighbors. *Examples:* Schedule potluck dinners, ice-cream socials, and other get-togethers to which young people may invite neighbors.

✪ Be a positive presence in your neighborhood. *Examples:* Sponsor a neighborhood social for adults and young people; start a drop-in childcare center; start an after-school program; provide opportunities for kids and teens to serve the neighborhood.

ASSET #5
Caring School Climate

Kids feel that their school supports them, encourages them, and cares about them.

35% of the kids we surveyed have this asset in their lives.

At Home

○ Ask your children how they feel about school. Do they perceive it as a caring, nurturing place? Why or why not? Encourage them to give specific reasons for the way they feel.

○ Have your child share the names of people at school who show that they care about students. Write a personal note of thanks and appreciation to everyone your child names— perhaps with your child's help and input.

○ Get involved with a parent-teacher organization. Work to create a spirit of cooperation.

○ Invite your child's teacher(s) to dinner at your home.

○ Volunteer at your child's school. *Examples:* Help out in the classroom; tutor kids in reading or math; spend time in the library or media center; chaperone field trips and school events.

○ Thank your children's teachers for the good work they do.

At School

☺ Don't tolerate bullying or disrespect of any kind. Insist on an atmosphere of kindness and mutual respect, and make these expectations clear.

☺ Learn the names of as many students as you can. Smile at them and greet them by name when you see them.

☺ Start a lunchtime, study-hall, or after-school discussion group for students who want to "just talk."

☺ Get to know your students on a personal level. Ask them about their interests, hobbies, passions, goals, hopes, and dreams.

☺ Nurture a sense of school ownership in students by involving them in decision making. *Examples:* Suggest that students create their own list of class or school rules; invite their input on ways to improve the cafeteria, gym, school grounds, or media center; form student committees to address specific problems.

☺ Create an environment where everyone—students, teachers, administrators, staff, visitors, parents, and other volunteers—feels welcome.

☺ Plan extracurricular activities that bring students, teachers, administrators, and staff together for fun and fellowship.

☺ Conduct a schoolwide survey to learn students' opinions about the school climate. Work with students to frame the questions and the look of the survey. Questions might include "What do you like best about our school?" "What do you like least about our school?" "What would you change to make our school more caring?" Tabulate and publicize the results. Form student-teacher-staff

committees to address areas of concern and implement
ideas gathered from the surveys.

In the Community

○ Support your local schools. Acknowledge and honor those
known for their caring climates. Vote yes for referendums
that reduce class sizes and improve facilities.

○ Feature caring schools, teachers, and administrators in
newspaper articles, on local television programs, and on
community websites.

○ Hold community forums on the topic of caring schools.
Invite school administrators to attend. Ask residents for
recommendations on how local schools can support and
nurture students.

○ Encourage all adults to volunteer in the schools, not just
parents of students.

In the Faith Community

○ Hold roundtable discussions on the topic of caring schools.
Invite parents and kids to share their ideas and concerns.
Summarize them and communicate them to area schools.

○ Identify the teachers, school administrators, and other
educators among your membership. Acknowledge and
honor their efforts.

○ Encourage members to volunteer in schools.

○ When the youth group looks for service projects, don't
forget about nearby schools. *Examples:* Young people might
volunteer to paint, remove graffiti, work on the grounds,
make repairs, tutor students, or help out in other ways.

ASSET #6
Parent Involvement in Schooling

Parents are actively involved in helping young people succeed in school. They talk with their kids about school, sometimes assist with schoolwork, and attend school events.

33% of the kids we surveyed have this asset in their lives.

At Home

- Speak with each of your child's teachers in person at least once during the school year. Email or call to check in every other month.

- Regularly ask your kids what they are learning about in school. Offer to help with homework in appropriate ways. *Example:* It's okay to help a child plan a special paper, and to be available for advice, suggestions, or rides to the library. It's *not* okay to write the paper.

- When you receive a school calendar, enter important dates and events onto your family calendar. Make attending school events a family priority.

○ Join the parent-teacher organization at your child's school. If you can't volunteer a lot of time, say so, but try to attend meetings.

○ Volunteer to do what you can to help out at your child's school. *Examples:* Be a room parent, chaperone school functions, serve on committees.

○ If you're concerned about circumstances or events at your child's school, talk to teachers and administrators. If you feel that you're not being heard, talk to other parents about constructive ways to address your concerns.

○ In general, parents tend to be most involved with their children's education during elementary school and less involved during middle and high school. Make it a point to stay actively involved for as long as your child is in school.

At School

○ Personally contact each student's family at least once during the school year.

○ Form a parent advisory committee to provide input and feedback on school policy decisions.

○ Send notes home to parents frequently about what students are working on and learning in class.

○ If you publish a class newsletter, print additional copies for your students to take home to their parents. Or start a class website and share the link with parents.

○ Start a website or email list specifically devoted to school events, and make sure that parents and families feel welcome to attend and participate.

In the Community

○ When possible, coordinate activities with the school(s) so parents and kids don't have to choose between school events and community events.

○ On days when schools have open houses and parent-teacher conferences, provide activities for younger children so parents are free to participate without childcare concerns.

○ Allow and encourage employees to volunteer time at schools.

In the Faith Community

○ When possible, don't schedule activities for young people that conflict with important school activities.

○ Encourage parents to show an interest in their children's school experience and to take any concerns they have to the school.

○ Offer workshops for parents on how to get involved and stay involved in their children's schools.

ASSET BUILDING
IN ACTION

Colorado parent and educator Lynn Stambaugh believes passionately that a healthy community starts with responsible and caring adults. She also recognizes the importance of these adults in young people's lives. One year, she drew up a list of all the adults who interact regularly with her kids—not just teachers, but coaches, janitors, bus drivers, music teachers, and others. She wrote each of them a letter:

"As an adult working with young people, you play a very important role in [their] lives . . . [during] these 'very hard to grow up' years." Then she described the Developmental Assets and said, "You make a difference. Thank you for your hard work and your dedication."

The letters drew what Stambaugh called "an amazing response." Many recipients wrote or phoned to thank her. Others responded with special warmth to Stambaugh's four kids. Stambaugh reflects, "The letters were great because they opened up communication between families and other adults involved in kids' lives."

Tips for Teens

Build Your Own Assets

Asset #1: Family Support

GOAL: *A family that is loving and supportive, and a home that is a comfortable place to be*

If you want your home to be warm, caring, comfortable, supportive, and fun, do your part to make it that way. Replace put-downs with kind words, teasing with supporting, thinking "me" with thinking "we." Show some affection, show some interest, and really listen when other people want to talk. Treat the people in your family the way you would like them to treat you. These ideas may sound simple, but they can make a big difference.

Asset #2: Positive Family Communication

GOAL: *Parents you can turn to for advice, support, and in-depth conversations about serious issues*

When you ask your parents for advice or support, do you feel like you get a lecture in response? For most parents, giving advice is an almost irresistible urge. You might try explaining that sometimes all you really need them to do is listen while you sort things out. Or suggest a compromise: You talk, they listen, and 10 minutes later (or an hour, or a day) you listen to what they have to say.

Here's another idea you might want to try: Find things your parents are really good at, and focus on those. *Examples:* If your mom is a math whiz, turn to her when you're worried about the math final. If your dad likes to write, ask for his advice on the article you're writing for your school newspaper.

If you feel that you can't talk to your parents about serious things, maybe it's because they still treat you like a child. Sometimes it's hard for parents to accept that children grow up and form their own beliefs and opinions. If there's another adult in your life you can talk to—someone who values your opinions and treats you with respect—try to arrange a meeting between you, your parents, and the other adult. Maybe your parents will see you through that person's eyes.

It's normal for kids and parents to disagree. Try to stay calm, and keep your voice down. Meanwhile, make an effort to see your parents' point of view. You'll be setting a good example for them to follow.

Asset #3: Other Adult Relationships

GOAL: *Three or more adults besides your parents you can turn to for advice, support, and in-depth conversations about serious issues*

If you don't have other adults to talk to, start looking in the places you normally go—your school, place of worship, scout troop, neighborhood park, or community center. You'll probably find adults who enjoy spending time with young people. Or see if there's a teen clinic in your area. Most (if not all) offer counseling, not just medical advice.

Join an adult-sponsored group, troop, or team. Meet your neighbors. Talk to your school counselor, have a heart-to-heart with a favorite aunt or uncle, or get to know your friends' parents. Form a relationship with a mentor in your community, faith community, or youth program. If you're willing to reach out, you *will* find adults you can talk to.

Asset #4: Caring Neighborhood

GOAL: *Neighbors who support you, encourage you, and care about you*

You can do a lot to create a caring neighborhood. Start by introducing yourself to adults you see, as well as to people your age. Say hi to younger kids, too. Be a friend and role model to them.

Get to know your neighbors. Smile at them and greet them when you see them on the street. When you can, spend a few moments talking with them. If you notice that they need assistance—carrying groceries, opening a door, hauling a stroller up the stairs—offer your help. Ask a neighbor to teach you something, such as how to bake bread or change a tire. Find out about neighborhood events (block parties, socials) and get involved.

It's likely that many people in your neighborhood don't know the children and teenagers who live there. You can help your neighborhood become more kid-friendly by creating a newsletter that gives some basic information about the events and people in your neighborhood. Ask younger children to help you gather the information; ask other teenagers to help produce the newsletter; ask kids to help distribute the newsletter to every home. Make sure that you know the names of everyone on your block or in your building.

Be aware that some adults are intimidated by groups of kids, especially teenagers. If you and several friends are walking down the street and you see a neighbor you know, stop and say hello. If you're walking toward each other, don't make your neighbor walk around you. Move out of the way so he or she can pass comfortably.

Asset #5: Caring School Climate

GOAL: *A school where you feel cared about, encouraged, and supported*

When you're involved in school activities, you're more likely to feel cared about and supported than if you're on the outside looking in. Try out for a team, run for student council, join a club, write for the school paper, join (or start) a service group. There may be many more ways to get involved than you realize, so if you're not sure what opportunities exist in your school, ask a teacher or administrator.

Do your part to treat other students well. Help them feel cared about and supported. Reach out to kids who seem isolated or lonely and aren't included in cliques or groups. When you're choosing teams for gym class activities or after-school sports, don't just choose your friends. Make it clear that you won't tolerate bullying of any kind, and stick up for kids who are targeted for bullying by others. Respect school property and encourage other students to do the same.

Encourage your parents to volunteer in your school. Schools become stronger and more caring when parents are active and informed.

Asset #6: Parent Involvement in Schooling

GOAL: *Parents who are actively involved in helping you succeed in school*

Talk to your parents about school. Tell them about your day, your successes, your frustrations. Share funny stories with them. Ask them to help you with a school project or a tricky homework problem.

If your teachers send notes, schedules, and announcements home with you, be sure to give them to your parents. Offer to write important school events on the family calendar. Remind your parents of special events a few days in advance. Let them know that you really *want* them to be involved.

EMPOWERMENT

Young people need to be empowered. They must be valued by their community and have opportunities to contribute to the well-being of others. For this to occur, they must be safe and feel secure.

The four **empowerment assets** are:

7. Community Values Youth

8. Youth as Resources

9. Service to Others

10. Safety

The more a young person is valued and feels valuable—and therefore empowered—the more likely it is that she or he will grow up healthy.

ASSET #7
Community Values Youth

Kids perceive that adults in the community value young people.

25% of the kids we surveyed have this asset in their lives.

At Home

✪ Ask your kids what makes them feel valued. *Tips:* Children and teens feel valued when (1) adults take time to be with them; (2) adults listen to them and take seriously what they have to say; and (3) adults seek them out and solicit their feedback.

✪ Point out to your children how your town or city currently uses resources to help kids prosper. *Examples:* parks, recreation programs, youth programs. Ask if they have ideas about how your community could do more.

✪ Talk with your children about where they feel valued in the community and where they don't. Ask them for specific reasons and examples. Encourage them to spend most of their time in places where they feel valued.

✪ Have regular family meetings to plan, solve problems, and encourage each other. Rotate who leads the meetings.

- Role-play positive and appropriate ways for kids to respond when community members treat them disrespectfully.
- Attend community events as a family. You'll improve your child's perceptions of your community—and vice versa.
- Affirm and support your children's friends. Let them know that you value them.

At School

- Ask students to create pictures or stories of what a community looks and feels like when it values young people. With students' permission, disseminate these pictures and stories at school and beyond.
- Form partnerships with community organizations through which students can volunteer and/or develop mentoring relationships with adults.
- Invite community members to a school open house hosted by students. Invite neighbors to functions that showcase students' work and creativity. *Examples:* school plays, science fairs, athletic events.
- Regularly invite people from the community to speak to students about careers, volunteer activities, and other areas of interest.
- Encourage students to get involved in community service.
- Create leadership roles for young people. Are there students on your school board? Do students sit on decision-making committees?

In the Community

✪ Instead of viewing kids as problems, start viewing them as assets.

✪ Use focus groups to find out (1) how kids think the community perceives them and (2) how they feel they are treated by adults in the community. Identify and target problem areas and celebrate successes.

✪ Educate adults in ways to show kids they matter. (See the tips in the first bullet under "At Home," page 60.)

✪ Encourage youth involvement in neighborhood and community organizations.

✪ Give positive feedback to young people you encounter in stores and other businesses (as clerks, sales help, waitstaff, and so on) when you notice them doing a good job.

✪ Publicize and celebrate the ways young people contribute to the community.

✪ Challenge negative stereotypes of young people in the media.

✪ Display youth artwork and projects at local stores, community centers, and other places where community members are likely to see them.

✪ Thank people who work with children and teens (such as teachers, youth group leaders, social service providers, and clergy). Show that you value them, too.

In the Faith Community

✪ Welcome kids and teens as part of the faith community, rather than as a separate group. Give them meaningful roles—as greeters, ushers, teachers for younger kids—and recognize them for their contributions.

✪ Include young people in leadership so they are valued by the members of the faith community.

✪ Maintain year-round connections with young people. Don't lose contact over the summer.

✪ Form a committee, made up of kids and teens, to discuss youth issues and to seek solutions to challenges facing young people.

✪ Educate members about negative stereotypes of young people. Brainstorm ways for kids *and* adults to overcome these stereotypes.

ASSET #8
Youth as Resources

Kids are given useful roles in the community.

32% of the kids we surveyed have this asset in their lives.

At Home

○ Involve your children in family decisions. Ask for their input and advice. Take their interests, talents, and opinions seriously.

○ Have a family meeting and get everyone's ideas on the best ways to accomplish household tasks. Share the decisions and share the work.

○ Ask your children to help you plan family reunions, family outings, or neighborhood gatherings.

○ Provide your children with age-appropriate roles that contribute to your family's well-being. *Examples:* planning and preparing meals, doing meaningful chores, helping younger siblings with homework, helping adults with significant tasks. Remind them often that their roles are important to the family as a whole.

○ Instead of only *buying* gifts for birthdays and holidays, commission your children to make some gifts.

○ Use some of your home projects as teaching opportunities. *Examples:* With your child, build a birdhouse, fix a bike, paint a room, or plant a garden.

○ Ask your child to teach you something—current slang, tips for navigating the Internet, a hobby, a song, how to play a video game.

○ Talk with your kids about their talents and abilities. What do *they* think they're good at? What do *you* think they're good at? Together, come up with ways they can share their gifts with others.

At School

○ Include students in school decision making. *Examples:* Students might sit on planning committees, produce the school handbook, or prepare the program for the annual open house.

○ Teach young people how to positively exert their influence in community affairs. *Examples:* Teach them specific social action skills including telephoning, surveying, polling, and speechmaking.

○ Give student councils real authority over appropriate issues.

○ Engage young people as active planners in some aspects of their education. *Example:* Let students choose independent study projects or report topics.

○ Have students work together to develop a proposal for an extracurricular activity they would like to see available at their school.

✪ Empower kids and teens by teaching them how to teach others. *Examples:* Older students might tutor, read to, or develop mentoring relationships with younger students. Peers might teach peers. Offer extra credit to kids who teach or help other students.

✪ Cultivate leadership skills in many students, not just a select few.

In the Community

✪ Work to encourage the perception that young people are *resources* with skills, talents, and abilities to be tapped, as opposed to *problems* to be controlled.

✪ Train community agencies, neighborhood groups, and programs in ways to increase youth involvement in decision making.

✪ Include young people on neighborhood and community boards and councils. Give them opportunities to take leadership roles and make real contributions.

✪ Get kids and teens involved in your organization or business.

✪ Publicize volunteer programs and opportunities for young people.

✪ Create win-win situations for adults and young people working together. Make sure all sides at all levels see the benefits of cooperation and collaboration.

✪ Hire young people when appropriate. *Example:* You might hire students to create and update city and community websites or to serve as election judges.

In the Faith Community

○ Ask for youth input in faith community decisions.

○ Provide many opportunities for children and teens to be leaders in and contributors to the faith community. Regularly include them as leaders of worship services and other intergenerational events.

○ Revise your planning process as needed to include kids and teens as vision bearers, idea makers, speakers, and other important roles.

○ Involve teens in caring for and teaching younger children.

○ Include young people on volunteer committees.

ASSET #9
Service to Others

*Kids serve in the community
one hour or more per week.*

50% of the kids we surveyed have this asset in their lives.

At Home

✪ Be a role model for your children by serving others.

✪ Set aside two hours some weekend for serving others as a family. *Examples:* Pick up litter in a park; volunteer at a soup kitchen or shelter.

✪ Brainstorm at least 10 ways your family can serve others. Vote on one to do, pick a date, and do it. Afterward, talk about your experience. *Tip:* You don't need to commit to a large project. Service can be as simple as visiting someone who's homebound or baking cookies for the family across the hall.

✪ Together with your child, help a neighbor. *Examples:* Shovel snow for an elderly person; offer to take a child to the library or playground.

✪ Talk with your children about the benefits of serving others. These include (1) personal satisfaction, (2) learning to get along better with others, (3) acquiring new skills, (4) coming into contact with many different kinds of people, (5) learning patience, and (6) making a difference in the world.

✪ Encourage your kids to participate in service activities through school, youth organizations, or a faith community.

At School

✪ Include service learning as part of the regular school curriculum.

✪ Place as much emphasis on celebrating service as on rewarding athletic or academic achievement. *Examples:* Hold awards ceremonies for students who serve; publish articles about them in the school newspaper; give "service letters" and scholarships.

✪ Invite students to discuss the issues in your community—or in the world—they would like to help address. Once you have a list, brainstorm ways to tackle these challenges through service.

✪ Train teens in how to help, tutor, and befriend younger children.

✪ Invite local residents to serve your school. *Examples:* Neighbors might tutor students, mentor them, read to them, or sit with young kids at lunchtime.

✪ Encourage student groups to serve the school neighborhood.

✪ Have students collect items for distribution to needy families in your neighborhood or community.

In the Community

○ Create and publicize service opportunities for young people and families.

○ Ask kids how they would like to serve. Match opportunities to their interests and abilities.

○ Teach neighborhoods, faith communities, and civic organizations how to involve young people in service efforts.

○ Make volunteering convenient for children and teens. *Examples:* Schedule some service projects for after-school and weekend hours; provide transportation and adult supervision; donate needed supplies and building materials.

○ Recognize kids who serve. *Examples:* Praise them in community publications and/or on a community website; hold an annual awards banquet at your community center.

○ Create neighborhood service projects that bring adults and children together.

In the Faith Community

○ Make service a core value in your faith community. Speak of it often; write about it in publications and newsletters that go out to members; create flags and banners about it; honor members of all ages who serve.

○ Make service a central component of youth programming.

○ Create intergenerational service projects—opportunities for adults and kids to work together. Include kids and teens in service projects that the faith community undertakes as a whole.

○ Partner with a community agency that needs regular help and/or financial assistance. Engage members of all generations in that partnership.

○ Address social issues in youth education, and provide opportunities for young people to address those issues through service. *Examples:* hunger, illiteracy, homelessness.

ASSET #10
Safety

*Kids feel safe at home, at school,
and in their neighborhood.*

54% of the kids we surveyed have this
asset in their lives.

At Home

✪ Don't tolerate hurtful words or actions in your home.
Model loving, respectful behavior toward your spouse,
children, other family members, and friends.

✪ Set clear family ground rules about maintaining physical
and emotional safety within the family. Talk about things
that make people feel safe and unsafe. Seek professional
help if any family member violates the physical or
emotional safety of another.

✪ Establish simple but firm house rules about answering the
telephone, opening the door to strangers, spending time
at home alone, surfing the Internet, watching TV, using
appliances, and respecting curfews.

✪ Keep track of all family members' plans and whereabouts.
Let each other know about changes.

○ Together with your children, meet and get to know as many people in your neighborhood as possible. Watch out for their safety and ask them to do the same for you.

○ Work with your neighbors to address safety needs and concerns in the neighborhood.

○ Talk with your children about what to do if they feel unsafe at school, on the street, in the park, or anywhere they go. Make sure they understand that they can tell you about bad things that happen to them.

○ Walk or drive your children's friends home after dark, even if they live nearby.

At School

○ Make it a priority to create a safe environment in the school building, on school grounds, and at school activities. Ask kids what makes them feel unsafe at school, solicit their input on ways to make school safer, and act on their suggestions.

○ Don't tolerate bullying or disrespect of any kind. Insist on an atmosphere of kindness and mutual respect, and make these expectations clear.

○ Actively work to create an environment that accepts, welcomes, and celebrates diversity.

○ Work to keep student-teacher ratios low so teachers can spend more time teaching and less time trying to manage students' behavior.

- Set and enforce a no-tolerance policy regarding weapons, violence, harassment, and discrimination. Establish an anonymous way for students to report when others violate these boundaries.
- Teach children how to tell adults about bad things that happen to them.
- Establish a peer mediation program so students can help each other resolve conflicts peacefully.
- Encourage teachers, administrators, and staff members to get to know students and to watch out for their safety.
- Provide information and training to students about how to protect their safety and the safety of others.

In the Community

- Meet with teenagers in your community to find out where they do and don't feel safe. Ask what could be done to help them feel safer.
- Provide young people with safe, supervised times and places where they can hang out with their friends.
- Make safety a high priority in parks and other public places.
- Coordinate residents to provide safe places where young people can go if they feel threatened.
- Promote and support neighborhood watch programs, block clubs, D.A.R.E. (Drug Abuse Resistance Education), Safety Camp, National Night Out, and other crime-prevention, community-building efforts.

○ Make sure that kids and teens have access to services (such as hotlines and counselors) for times when their safety is violated.

In the Faith Community

○ Create a safe environment for young people in the faith community. Monitor adults who work with kids and teens, and avoid situations where safety could be compromised.

○ Make your building a safe haven for kids in trouble.

○ Educate the entire faith community on how members can help young people feel safe at home, at school, and in their community.

○ Work for community change that can make neighborhoods safer for children and teens.

ASSET BUILDING
IN ACTION

In Basking Ridge, New Jersey, young people took the lead in making their community asset-rich. Through the local Somerset Hills YMCA, they were at the forefront of two Developmental Assets initiatives.

The first of these initiatives was an asset-building speakers' bureau. One year, kids led in-service training for teachers in the Somerset Hills School District. They also trained the YMCA Board of Directors, the Bernardsville Chamber of Commerce, the YMCA staff, and the Bernardsville Town Council. "This is really about flipping things upside down," said Carolyn Vasquez, YMCA community outreach director. "The kids are teaching the adults."

Young people also took the asset message into the community by doing an Asset Mapping Program. They visited local businesses, restaurants, and community organizations to educate people about the Developmental Assets and to help them take a Developmental Assets inventory. Through the mapping project, young people showed community members how to take a more intentional approach to asset building.

Vasquez reports that this project of community building through the assets has had a positive impact. Local young people "are more aware of their community as a whole," she says. "They're becoming more involved little by little to create change."

Tips for Teens

Build Your Own Assets

Asset #7: Community Values Youth

GOAL: *A community where you feel and perceive that you and other young people are appreciated and valued*

Think about your experiences as a member of your community. Do you feel valued? Ignored? Appreciated? Scorned? Invisible? Why do you feel the way you do? Are there certain people in your community who make you feel worthwhile—and others who make you feel worthless? What can you do to improve the way you and other teens are perceived and treated in your community?

You might start by showing that you value your community. Get involved in a neighborhood project, for example. When you notice adults negatively stereotyping young people, question them about their views. In response, offer examples of children and teens who are actively working to make the community a better place. Don't be too shy to speak proudly about the ways you're contributing to your community . . . or, if you really don't want to talk about yourself, then speak proudly about your friends.

Sometimes we don't realize how much other people value us. You might want to identify four adults you know (like a parent, another adult relative, a neighbor, teacher, or coach) and ask each one what he or she thinks of you. Do they see you as an important member of the community? If so, why? Their answers may surprise you.

Asset #8: Youth as Resources

GOAL: *A community where you and other young people have useful roles and meaningful things to do*

Look around your community and learn about the many opportunities available to give something back. Where can you contribute? Where can you lead? Can you be an officer in a school club or youth organization? Can you run for student council? Are there neighborhood, town, or city councils or committees that welcome youth involvement? (If they don't welcome it yet, they might with a little encouragement.)

Don't wait around to be "given" a useful role. Instead, create one for yourself. Stand up, speak out, and stay informed. Write letters to the editor of your local newspaper on issues that concern you. Lobby for (or against) area ordinances or laws. Give a speech on a topic you care about—children's rights, homelessness, bullying in schools, domestic violence, senior citizens, healthcare. Develop a skill you can share with and teach to others. Become an expert on a topic that's important to you—computers, cats, clean water, recycling—and educate others. Campaign for someone who's running for office in your school, city, or state. It's your community, too, and you have the right to be an active, important part of it.

Get other kids involved in your efforts and offer them useful roles. For instance, if you're campaigning for a candidate, they can help you hand out flyers. Younger kids love it when older, wiser kids take them seriously and make them feel wanted and needed.

Asset #9: Service to Others

GOAL: *To serve in your community one hour or more per week*

Serving in your community is a great way to meet people and find new meaning in life. There are countless ways to serve. Think about your friends, people in your neighborhood, homeless people, elderly people, animals, the environment, your school, your faith community, your youth organization . . . what else? Figure out where you want to serve, then find out what's needed and how you can do the most good. One hour per week is almost no time at all; you probably spend at least that long surfing the Internet, watching TV, or just hanging out.

If you want to find out how good it feels to serve but you're not quite ready to commit, try this: Do a "secret service" for someone you know. Take out the trash when it's your brother's turn. Leave a treat in a friend's locker or a potted plant on a neighbor's porch. Or talk to people who are active in community service. Ask them what they give—and what they get in return.

If you're not sure where to start serving, check online or in the phone book to see if any of the following organizations have chapters near you. Many welcome young people and give them opportunities to serve.

- Boys & Girls Clubs of America
- Boy Scouts of America
- Girls Inc.
- Girl Scouts of the U.S.A.
- Habitat for Humanity
- Kids Against Crime
- Kids for Saving Earth
- National Youth Advisory Council

- Students Against Destructive Decisions (SADD)

- United Way
- Youth Service America

Asset #10: Safety

GOAL: *To feel safe at home, at school, and in your neighborhood*

Tell your parents about any fears or concerns you have—about your home, neighborhood, parks, school, or anyplace else you go. Describe any events that have made you feel worried or afraid. Ask for help from your parents, teachers, religious leaders, or other adults you know and trust. When you live in fear, you're less likely to take healthy risks, try new things, and make positive contributions. You're also less likely to succeed at school. If school feels unsafe to you, you might encourage your parents to volunteer at your school and see for themselves what it's like. Then you can talk about ideas for improving your school's environment.

Do your part to make your neighborhood, community, and school safer for everyone. Start or join a group, brainstorm ideas, and volunteer to help put your ideas into action. Or choose an issue that interests you and promote safety. *Examples:* crime prevention, accident prevention, disease prevention, emergency first aid, disaster prevention and preparation. You might educate others about fire prevention, bicycle helmets, or emergency services in your community. Suggest that your school or community hold a safety fair, or ask your mayor to proclaim a Safety Week for your town or city. When you work for safety, everyone benefits—including you.

BOUNDARIES and EXPECTATIONS

Young people need to know what is expected of them and whether activities and behaviors are "in bounds" or "out of bounds."

The six **boundaries and expectations assets** are:

11. Family Boundaries

12. School Boundaries

13. Neighborhood Boundaries

14. Adult Role Models

15. Positive Peer Influence

16. High Expectations

The more a young person has clear, consistent boundaries and high expectations, the more likely it is that he or she will grow up healthy.

ASSET #11
Family Boundaries

Parents set clear rules and consequences for their kids' behavior. They monitor their children's whereabouts.

47% of the kids we surveyed have this asset in their lives.

At Home

☢ Talk with your spouse or partner about boundaries for your children's behavior, and reach agreement. Kids need parents to stand together.

☢ Talk with your children about your family's boundaries. Be positive; say what you *want* them to do, not just what you *don't want* them to do. Make boundaries clear and concise—five words or less, if possible.

☢ Once you've articulated your family boundaries, expect your children to honor them. Don't suspect them of misbehavior without a reason.

☢ Meet monthly to discuss boundaries. Are they fair? Do they still fit? Do they reflect your family's values and principles? Adjust them if you need to. If you need help, read parenting books and seek advice. Be willing to learn and change.

✪ Regularly renegotiate family rules with teenagers so they're developmentally appropriate—but know that even 18-year-olds still need boundaries.

✪ Focus discipline as a way to teach, not as a form of punishment. Never let discipline become an excuse for venting anger. If you need help, call a local crisis hotline and ask for information on support groups for parents.

✪ Have a family calendar on which all family members (including parents) note where they will be and when.

✪ Learn who your children's friends are, then invite their parents to form a "parent network" with you. Agree that children will not be allowed to hold or attend parties without adult supervision.

✪ Make your home an inviting place for your kids and their friends. When they're home, you know where they are!

At School

✪ Respect and reinforce family values and rules as much as possible.

✪ Talk with parents about their standards for their children's conduct, and share with them your standards for student conduct. Find common ground and support each other's efforts.

✪ Include parents in meetings with students regarding problem behaviors and broken rules.

In the Community

❂ Offer workshops for parents on ways to establish boundaries, address problem behaviors, and enforce consequences. Invite experts to speak and field questions.

❂ Offer support groups so parents can learn from each other about establishing and enforcing appropriate family boundaries.

❂ As you set standards for young people's participation in community activities, invite parents to contribute their ideas and suggestions.

❂ Create tip sheets for parents on fair and effective discipline strategies.

❂ Gather a list of resources—such as books, websites, videos, and podcasts—that provide clear, helpful tips for parents. Publish this list on a community website or in a newsletter.

❂ Create a form for kids and parents on which everyone agrees to let each other know about their whereabouts. Publicize the form, post it on a community website, introduce it at a local meeting, and have copies of the form available to community parents.

❂ When you see young people in inappropriate places, take responsibility to ask them whether their parents know where they are.

In the Faith Community

✪ Set and enforce clear expectations for the behavior of the young people in your faith community.

✪ Educate parents in how to set appropriate boundaries. Include ideas in worship bulletins and mailings to member households.

✪ Give parents opportunities to talk together about family boundaries.

✪ Educate young people about how to set boundaries for themselves. This would be an excellent topic for a youth retreat.

✪ Provide adequate adult supervision for all youth group events.

ASSET #12
School Boundaries

Schools set clear rules and consequences for student behavior.

56% of the kids we surveyed have this asset in their lives.

At Home

✪ Encourage your child's school to create a code of conduct at the beginning of the year, review the code with the students, and send copies home to families. Volunteer to help with this process, and suggest that students play a role in creating the code.

✪ Get involved in a parent-teacher policy organization.

✪ Inform yourself about school boundaries by visiting your child's school. Observe how students behave, how adults and students interact with each other, and how conflicts are resolved. If you have questions, take them to your child's teachers or the school principal.

✪ Talk with your child's teachers about boundaries in the classroom. Talk with your child about the importance of respecting those boundaries. If there are some your child doesn't agree with, find out why.

○ Take time to learn about and discuss school boundaries as a family each school year.

○ Support school boundaries, consequences, and expectations for students' behavior.

○ Contact school authorities if you learn that school boundaries are not being enforced fairly, consistently, or appropriately.

○ When conflicts occur, don't be pushy. Calmly state your concern and suggest solutions.

At School

○ Create an official school policy on behaviors that are in-bounds (*examples:* learning, caring, respecting differences) and out-of-bounds (*examples:* bullying, violence, cheating, harassment). Establish clear consequences for out-of-bounds behaviors—and ways to affirm in-bounds behaviors. Involve students, parents, and staff in creating this policy. Review it several times a year with everyone in the school community.

○ If you publish a student handbook, send copies home to parents.

○ Include young people in establishing boundaries and communicating them to other students.

○ Expect young people to behave responsibly. When they don't, enforce consequences fairly and consistently.

○ Post your school boundaries in many places throughout the school—classrooms, halls, cafeteria, auditorium.

○ Use peer mediation as one way to resolve boundary violations.

- Notice and celebrate students who consistently follow school policies and respect school boundaries.
- Provide adequate adult supervision in the lunchroom, in the hallways, on the playground, and other places where students gather.

In the Community

- Support school leaders in developing, communicating, and enforcing school boundaries.
- As much as possible, make sure that school boundaries are consistent from school to school.
- Talk publicly about school boundaries. Let the community know about them so they can support and reinforce them. Post flyers, send mailings, add information to a community website, and/or present the boundaries at an open house.
- Be sure that coaches and other adult leaders (of teams, clubs, youth organizations, extracurricular activities, after-school programs, and so on) are informed of school boundaries. Ask for their support in enforcing them.

In the Faith Community

- Learn what the boundaries are in your community's schools. Summarize and publicize them in worship bulletins and mailings to member households. Encourage parents to support them.
- Work with schools to define common boundaries that may be taught at school and in the faith community.
- Find out about school policies for student behavior. Reinforce those expectations within the faith community.

ASSET #13
Neighborhood Boundaries

Neighbors take responsibility for monitoring young people's behavior.

48% of the kids we surveyed have this asset in their lives.

At Home

○ Hold a front-yard barbecue, block party, or building party to connect with neighbors. Discuss neighborhood boundaries and identify three or more that everyone can agree on. *Examples:* Respect people and property; report suspicious activity; supervise children younger than 16; end parties by a certain agreed-upon time; talk to neighbors directly about concerns. Publish the boundaries in a one-page newsletter and distribute it door-to-door, or post a list of these boundaries on your neighborhood website.

○ As a neighborhood, encourage each other to point out boundaries to kids and teens. *Example:* If a neighbor hears young people swearing, everyone should support the neighbor saying "We don't use that kind of language in our neighborhood."

○ Notice daily what happens in your neighborhood.

○ Talk with your children about neighborhood boundaries.

○ Call other neighbors about concerns or questions. Distribute a neighborhood directory with names, phone numbers, and addresses of neighbors who are interested in participating.

○ Invite neighbors you trust to tell you when they notice your child behaving inappropriately. Let your child know that you have done this. Encourage neighbors to affirm positive behaviors, too.

○ Establish and enforce clear boundaries for young people who visit your home.

○ Welcome new neighbors and introduce them to your neighborhood's boundaries. Invite their suggestions and support.

At School

○ Talk with students about neighborhood boundaries. Do their neighborhoods have boundaries for young people's behavior? How do they know? Which neighbors seem to notice and care about what they do? How do they (the students) feel about that? Ask students to identify neighbors they perceive as especially caring. They might want to write thank-you notes.

○ Find out what boundaries exist in your school's neighborhood—or set reasonable boundaries and communicate them to students. *Examples:* no littering, no cutting across neighbors' lawns, no loitering on private property, no booming car stereos. Let neighbors know that you have done this.

⊙ Survey the school neighborhood to learn if neighbors have any concerns or complaints about student behavior. Communicate these to students and set boundaries to address them.

In the Community

⊙ Work to create strong neighborhood bonds. Sponsor activities that encourage neighbors to get to know each other better.

⊙ Work with others in the community (individuals, groups, and organizations) to identify and articulate community norms and standards. Include young people in this process.

⊙ Work with local businesses, neighborhood organizations, and law enforcement agencies to identify places where kids get into trouble. Start a series of community meetings to brainstorm and implement solutions.

⊙ Involve kids and teens in establishing boundaries for public places. *Examples:* parks, playgrounds, shopping malls, community centers. Display flyers or posters listing the boundaries in clear, concise language.

⊙ Expect young people to behave responsibly. When they don't, enforce boundaries appropriately.

⊙ Enforce curfew laws.

In the Faith Community

✪ Set and enforce clear boundaries for kids and teens in the faith community.

✪ When young people behave inappropriately, let them know that you've noticed—and that you expect more of them.

✪ Teach adults in the faith community about the importance of neighborhood boundaries for kids. Encourage them to get to know their neighbors and to work with them to establish neighborhood boundaries.

✪ Be an active part of your faith community's neighborhood, even if not all members live in the vicinity. Be aware of the neighborhood's boundaries and encourage the faith community's members to respect them.

ASSET #14
Adult Role Models

*Parents and other adults model positive,
responsible behavior.*

28% of the kids we surveyed have this
asset in their lives.

At Home

✪ Always remember that *you* are your child's most important
role model. Set high standards for yourself and follow
them—even during difficult times. Treat your child with
love and respect.

✪ Be involved in your child's life on a daily basis. Spend time
together often. Take advantage of "teachable moments"—
times and events that invite discussion and learning about
positive, responsible behavior.

✪ Talk with your children about adults they know who are
positive role models. Find ways to build and strengthen
those relationships. Invite friends you respect, admire, and
trust to get involved in your children's lives.

✪ Talk with your children about people you see on television
and websites, and in movies, magazines, and newspapers.
Discuss whether they are good role models, and why or
why not. Talk about the differences between role models
and celebrities.

✪ Talk with your children about your own role models. Who do you admire, and why? Who were your role models when you were a child? A teenager? A young adult?

✪ Talk honestly about the issues when you or another adult lets your child down. It's also good role-modeling to apologize for failures and admit mistakes.

At School

✪ Educate *all* staff about the importance of modeling positive, responsible behavior.

✪ Make an extra effort to notice and affirm a diverse range of adult role models, including people of different genders, ages, ethnicities, and faiths.

✪ Have students identify their heroes. Discuss whether they are good role models. If they are, why? If they aren't, why not? Talk about the differences between heroes and celebrities.

✪ Focus on positive role models in history, literature, and other subjects.

✪ Expose students to positive adult role models in the community. Invite them into the classroom and school to talk about their lives and interact with students.

✪ Teach students to analyze figures in the media and identify ways they are positive and/or negative role models.

In the Community

✪ Volunteer to work with or alongside young people who need positive role models.

✪ Celebrate positive role models in your community through media coverage.

✪ Encourage adults to become mentors for young people.

✪ Present a series of talks, films, or readings exploring positive (and negative, as appropriate) role models, and encourage young people to attend. Hold discussion sessions afterward to dig deeper into ideas and questions.

✪ Honor *all* adults—not just celebrities or powerful people—who exhibit the qualities that you seek to nurture in kids and teens.

✪ Encourage celebrities and other influential people in your community to model positive, responsible behavior. Remind them that they are role models, and that they can be real-life heroes by setting positive examples for young people.

In the Faith Community

✪ Encourage adults to model the kinds of behavior they expect from young people.

✪ Clearly articulate what's expected of *all* people in the faith community.

✪ Provide adult mentors for young people.

✪ Have kids identify role models from your faith tradition. What makes them good role models?

✪ Invite positive role models in the faith community to share their life stories with children and teens.

✪ Encourage adults to get involved with youth groups in your faith community.

✪ Plan intergenerational programs and events so kids can meet adult role models.

ASSET #15
Positive Peer Influence

Children's closest friends model responsible behavior. They are a good influence. They do well at school and stay away from risky behaviors such as alcohol and other drug use.

68% of the kids we surveyed have this asset in their lives.

At Home

✪ Invite your children's friends to spend time in your home. Make them feel welcome and try to get to know them. Include them in some of your family activities.

✪ Talk with your kids about their friends, and ask questions about them. Are they good students? What are their interests? Do they get along well with their parents? Try to find out what your children like about their friends.

✪ Affirm positive friendships without going overboard. *Example:* You might say, "Jeff seems like a nice kid. He's funny and easy to be around. I'm glad you invite him over."

○ Resist the urge to criticize friendships that seem negative. Many kids get defensive about friends their parents don't like. This often makes them even more determined to maintain the friendships.

○ Don't jump to conclusions based on what your child's friends look like.

○ Get to know the parents of your children's friends. Have your kids introduce you at school open houses, community meetings, or activities at your place of worship.

○ Children learn by example. Ask yourself: Do *your* friends model responsible behavior? Are they a good influence on you?

At School

○ Train students to be peer counselors or peer helpers. Choose kids who can become good role models and who are respected and liked by their peers.

○ Provide cooperative learning opportunities for students. Let students work together in groups. Make sure all children benefit from the experience. For example, the most accelerated students shouldn't spend all or most of their time tutoring other students.

○ Encourage students to form an after-school discussion club that focuses on friendship, peer pressure, and other related topics. Volunteer to be the club's faculty sponsor.

○ Use class time to teach about friendship. Challenge kids to think about their own friendships. Are they helpful or hurtful? How do they know? Help children develop the skills they need to make and keep good friends.

In the Community

✪ Provide opportunities for young people to model positive, responsible behavior for each other. *Examples:* Promote youth volunteer activities; encourage youth participation on community and city committees. Helping others through community service is one way to set a great example.

✪ Affirm and honor the healthful choices that young people make. *Examples:* Invite kids to create posters conveying messages against drug and alcohol use and/or violence, then sign them and display them in the community. Publish the names of honor students in local newspapers or on community websites. Encourage the media to profile young people who are making a difference in the community.

✪ Sponsor an awards night for young people in the community who serve as good role models. Community members could nominate deserving kids and teens by secret ballot.

In the Faith Community

✪ Start a peer support program. Train young people to be good listeners and to offer appropriate advice and suggestions. Teach them to know when and how to seek help from adults.

✪ Invite young people to think about ways to positively influence their friends and peers in school and in the community. This would be a great topic for a weekend youth retreat.

✪ Affirm and honor the young role models in your faith community.

✪ Make friendship a regular topic of discussion within your youth program. Ask kids about their friends. Ask them to think about how their friendships fit with their values.

✪ Sponsor youth events in which kids can include friends from outside the faith community.

ASSET #16
High Expectations

Parents and teachers encourage kids to do well.

55% of the kids we surveyed have this asset in their lives.

At Home

✪ Expect the best from your kids—each according to his or her unique abilities. Educate yourself on child development so you know what's realistic and how kids vary. When expectations are high yet still within reach, children will stretch to achieve them.

✪ Periodically revisit the expectations you have of your children, and modify them when necessary.

✪ Notice when your children do well. Let them know that you admire their talents, abilities, manners, friendship skills, intelligence, kindness, or whatever you happen to observe.

✪ Encourage both girls and boys to be independent.

✪ Hold kids accountable for their actions at the same time you affirm their abilities.

✪ Be on the lookout for new and creative ways to challenge and stimulate your children—without pushing too hard.

○ Ask your children what they expect of themselves. Listen closely and thoughtfully to what they say.

○ Let kids know that having high expectations isn't the same as expecting to be the best at everything.

○ Find and share inspiring stories about people who overcame obstacles in their lives and accomplished amazing things.

○ Encourage your children to tackle school subjects and out-of-school hobbies that are difficult for them. Work together.

○ Allow your children to make mistakes and to learn from them.

○ Model the benefits of high expectations by challenging yourself. Take a class, learn a skill, start a hobby, or stretch yourself in other ways.

At School

○ Tell students what you expect from them.

○ Talk with parents about expectations. Tell them what you expect from their children; ask them to share their expectations with you. Support each other.

○ Hold high expectations for *all* students, not just the stars. (Remember that "high" for one student may be "low" for another.)

○ Encourage students to take positive risks and to act on their dreams and ideas. Teach the difference between positive risks and foolish risks.

✪ Give students the tools they need to develop their talents and abilities.

✪ Give kids opportunities to sink or swim. They'll often rise to the occasion. *Example:* Don't always assume that an adult needs to direct an activity. Invite kids to lead and see what happens.

✪ Design learning opportunities that challenge students who have all types of learning styles and abilities.

In the Community

✪ Encourage adult leaders (such as coaches, choir directors, group leaders, and volunteer coordinators) to hold high expectations for *all* young people they work with, not just the stars.

✪ Challenge local media (TV, radio, newspapers, websites) to spotlight the positive accomplishments of many young people, as opposed to the negative actions of a few.

✪ Regularly recognize children and teens who excel in various areas—academics, sports, performance, service, leadership, creativity, courage.

✪ Reassure young people you come into contact with that they can do great things.

✪ Hold high expectations for young people in the workplace—whether you're an employer or a customer.

✪ Sponsor classes and workshops on child development so parents can learn how to set reasonable expectations.

In the Faith Community

○ Tell young people what you expect of them.

○ Hold high expectations for *all* kids and teens in your faith community.

○ Give young people opportunities to try new activities or build new skills. Let them know that you expect them to succeed.

○ Make religious education challenging and interesting.

○ Educate parents about how to set realistic yet encouraging expectations for their children.

ASSET BUILDING
IN ACTION

Principal Don MacIntyre decided to make asset building the foundation for McNicoll Park Middle School in Penticton, British Columbia. "I felt that creating a positive, supportive climate and culture in the school was the most important thing we could do," he said.

To build this climate, MacIntyre and the staff emphasized positive, productive behavior. They created schoolwide expectations that gave specific examples of how young people needed to act. For example, students were challenged in all settings to "be prepared to give your best effort, keep your hands and feet to yourself, and respect others' efforts and contributions."

Staff members started giving students "gotcha" tickets that rewarded students for "getting caught" displaying good behavior. The tickets went into a weekly drawing for prizes. "We have seen a consistent drop in the number of disciplinary referrals over the two-plus years that we have utilized this approach to dealing with student behavior," MacIntyre said.

"The students receive lots of support for doing the right things," MacIntrye said. "We thank them for meeting the school's expectations."

Tips for Teens
Build Your Own Assets

Asset #11: Family Boundaries

GOAL: *Parents who set clear rules and consequences for your behavior and monitor your whereabouts*

Boundaries, rules, expectations . . . who needs them? Actually, we all do. Life without them would be chaos. Boundaries guide us in making good decisions and provide structure for our everyday lives. Try thinking of boundaries as *positives* rather than negatives.

Talk with your parents about your family's boundaries. Do you respect, accept, and follow them? Why or why not? Do they seem reasonable to you—or totally unfair? Tell your parents how you feel and why. Listen to their side, too, and be respectful. If you can suggest alternatives or compromises, maybe your parents will try things your way. Meanwhile, if you break a rule, accept the consequences. This will *really* impress your parents.

If your parents drive you crazy with questions about where you're going, who with, what for, and how long, beat them to it. Give them the information they want *before* they ask for it. *Tip:* Put it in the form of a question. Instead of "Morgan and I are going to the 8:00 movie, then out to eat, and I'll be back by midnight," try saying "I'd like to go to the 8:00 movie with Morgan, then out to eat, and be back by midnight. Okay with you?" Then your parents can graciously give their permission. This way, everyone benefits. They get to feel generous, and you get to go out with your friend.

Asset #12: School Boundaries

GOAL: *A school that sets clear rules and consequences for students' behavior*

You have the right to attend a school where boundaries are clear and respected—a school where students are free to learn. If your school doesn't fit this description, do something about it.

Form a committee of other students who feel the way you do. Emphasize that the goal is not simply to make more rules. Instead, it's to define better and more helpful rules that benefit everyone. Find an adult sponsor—a teacher, coach, or school counselor—who's willing to work with you. Brainstorm a list of problems at your school. *Examples:* bullying, cheating, stealing, fighting, weapons, drugs, sexual harassment, racial discrimination, skipping class, students loitering in the halls, swearing. Then brainstorm fair and clear boundaries for each area—and reasonable consequences for infractions. Refine your lists and summarize your work in a Code of Conduct for your school. Present it to your principal and ask for his or her feedback. Work together on a final version. Make sure it's clear, and keep it as concise as you can—one page if possible. Send copies home to parents and post them throughout your school. Ask the principal if you can post the code of conduct on your school's website, too.

Or, if your school publishes a student handbook, you could start there. Is it too long, boring, or out of date? Does it address all of the problems or room for improvement that you see in your school? Your committee might work to revise the handbook.

Asset #13: Neighborhood Boundaries

GOAL: *Neighbors who take responsibility for monitoring your behavior*

Picture a neighborhood where people know each other and care about each other. Now picture a neighborhood where people are strangers. Which seems warmer and friendlier to you? Which seems safer? Where would you rather live?

You can help create a neighborhood where people watch out for each other—including you. Start by getting to know the people who live near you. Begin with the ones who seem friendly. Say hi and introduce yourself. The next time you see them, try a little conversation. You might ask them how long they've lived in the neighborhood and what they like about it. They might respond by asking you a question or two. Before you know it, you'll be talking together. Suggest that your parents meet your neighbors, too.

Meanwhile, get together with other teens and kids in your neighborhood. Help set neighborhood standards for safety, noise, or other issues. Agree to treat adults with respect. And start watching out for younger kids, too.

Asset #14: Adult Role Models

GOAL: *Parents and other adults who model positive, responsible behavior*

Who are the adult role models in your life? Think of three people you look up to. Include an adult family member (a parent, an adult sibling, an aunt, an uncle, a grandparent, or an adult cousin), a community member you know (a teacher, coach, neighbor, family friend, or youth group leader), and a national or world figure (a leader, a celebrity, an author, a historical figure, or someone else who's been in the news). Now think of why each person is a role model for you. Why do you admire her or him? What special qualities does each person have? Are these qualities that you have—or would like to have someday? How could you develop or strengthen these characteristics in yourself?

Ask adults you know and respect to describe their role models—people who have inspired them or influenced them in positive ways. You might want to learn more about those people or even meet them, if they live near you.

Choose your role models carefully. It's easy to pick famous people such as musicians, athletes, or actors. After all, they seem to be everywhere: on TV, on the Internet, on the radio, in magazines and advertisements. But before you decide to be like them, learn more about them. You might discover that the best role models are people you already know in your own life.

Asset #15: Positive Peer Influence

GOAL: *Friends who are responsible, who avoid risky behaviors, and who have a positive influence on you*

Think of your three or four closest friends—the people you spend the most time with and are most influenced by. Do they build you up or drag you down? Do you support each other in making good choices—even when bad choices are easily available? Only you know the answers to these questions. Forget about what your parents think or what other people say. How do *you* feel about the friends you have now? If you're not happy with your answer, there are places you can go to meet new people and eventually make new friends. Ask a trusted adult (parent, teacher, youth group leader) for suggestions.

You can also be a positive influence on your friends. When they start to take foolish risks or behave in other negative ways, don't go along. Be a peer helper and work to build assets in your friends and in yourself.

Asset #16: High Expectations

GOAL: *Parents and teachers who encourage you to do well*

Tell your parents your hopes and dreams; tell your teachers what you'd like to accomplish in their classes. Ask for their support. This encourages them to pay closer attention to your progress—and to set high expectations for you.

High expectations seem to bring out the best in all of us. When people we know and care about want us to do well, we try harder. High expectations boost our self-esteem. We feel more capable and willing to take positive risks. We're less afraid of making mistakes.

If you feel that your parents or teachers expect too little of you, talk with an adult you know and trust. It could be a youth leader, a neighbor, a school counselor, or an adult relative. Ask him or her for advice and insights. Maybe that person will offer to tell your parents and teachers what a wonderful person you really are and why they should have higher expectations for you.

You can also set high expectations for yourself. Many people have succeeded in life with little or no encouragement from others—and in spite of terrible odds and discouragement. *Tip:* Start a notebook of upbeat, inspiring quotations or sayings. Add to it regularly and refer to it when you're feeling down or doubtful about yourself.

CONSTRUCTIVE USE of TIME

Young people need constructive, enriching opportunities for growth through creative activities, youth programs, involvement in a faith community, and quality time at home.

The four **constructive use of time assets** are:

17. Creative Activities

18. Youth Programs

19. Religious Community

20. Time at Home

The more time a young person spends with caring adults who nurture his or her skills and creativity, the more likely it is that he or she will grow up healthy.

ASSET #17
Creative Activities

*Kids spend three or more hours
each week in lessons or practice in music,
theater, or other arts.*

20% of the kids we surveyed have this asset in their lives.

At Home

○ Encourage your kids to get involved with the arts. As much as possible, let them choose what to do—play an instrument, act or sing, dance, paint, write, draw, make pottery, or whatever interests them. Provide instruments, materials, and lessons (group lessons are fine). Allow and respect practice time.

○ Show your support by attending your children's performances, reading their writing, viewing their art, and so on. Notice and applaud their efforts.

○ Set some reasonable boundaries, but overall, don't complain when your teenager plays the drums for hours, emotes at the dining room table, sings in the shower, or splatters paint on the basement floor.

○ Make the arts a part of everyday life in your home. Explore different types of music; attend plays, musicals, concerts, dance performances, films, and operas as a family; visit art museums and cultural centers. Be sure to let your kids choose some of the activities.

✪ If you played an instrument when you were younger, take a refresher course. Then set a good example and practice often. Or join a choir, try out for a play, pick up a paintbrush, or write a poem. Share your excitement with your children.

✪ Be open to a wide variety of arts-related experiences. Scan the newspapers for notices of free performances. Encourage your children to keep you informed about school plays, band concerts, and art exhibits, and attend them as a family.

At School

✪ Provide free access to instruments, art materials, and lessons for students who can't afford them. If the school can't afford them, solicit donations from parents, the community, and local businesses.

✪ When school budgets are tight, music and the arts are among the first programs to be cut. Lobby hard to keep them at your school, or bring them back. Generate community support.

✪ Use music as a teaching tool in school curricula to reinforce and extend learning. Play background music during classes. While profiling famous people from history, include important musicians and play examples of their music. While exploring different cultures and languages, make music part of your lessons.

- Sponsor performances by local artists. Arrange for master classes, where performers share techniques and expertise with young people.

- Hold a school talent show and encourage a wide range of students to participate.

In the Community

- Sponsor youth bands, orchestras, drama clubs, dance troupes, and singing groups. Provide places to practice.

- Use local talent (youth orchestras, jazz bands, theater troupes, vocal ensembles, garage bands) at community functions. Invite artistic kids to create the banners, posters, and flyers advertising community events.

- Check with the schools to find out what they need for their arts programs. Audio equipment? Used musical instruments? Art supplies? Props for plays? Place articles in local newspapers urging community members to contribute.

- Sponsor free community events that expose young people (and their families) to a wide variety of arts performances.

- Promote appreciation for diversity by sponsoring world music concerts, ethnic dance performances, multicultural festivals, and other events.

In the Faith Community

- Form a youth band, choir, chorus, or other music group. Or include young people in adult groups.

✪ Especially during the summer months, when it's difficult to gather your complete choir, invite kids to perform solos, duets, or small ensemble pieces.

✪ Be open to featuring a variety of performances in your worship service—from music to skits, dances to poetry readings. Or schedule an all-arts service for one day or evening each month.

✪ Hold a faith community talent show, or put on a play. Encourage young people to join in.

✪ Encourage adults in the faith community to offer free lessons in the arts (*examples:* drawing, singing, piano, acting, dance) to young people as a ministry.

ASSET #18
Youth Programs

Kids spend three or more hours each week in sports, clubs, or other organizations at school and/or in the community.

61% of the kids we surveyed have this asset in their lives.

At Home

○ Talk with your children about their interests. Help them find teams, clubs, or other organizations that match or complement their interests. Encourage them to join one— and ask for a six-month commitment. Some kids drop out of programs prematurely, or they skip from one to another without giving any a real chance.

○ Become an adult leader at your child's school. Offer to sponsor or advise an existing school club. Or offer to sponsor a new club in an area that interests you. *Examples:* an amateur astronomers' club, photographers' club, writers' club, cooking club. If you can't volunteer your time, contribute what you can in terms of money or materials.

○ Start or join a car pool for kids who participate in extracurricular activities.

○ Set a good example by getting involved with a team, club, or organization that interests you.

At School

○ Offer extracurricular activities that appeal to a wide variety of needs and interests.

○ Create a clearinghouse of community youth activities. Post information about community activities on bulletin boards along with school activities. Call attention to them in your daily announcements and on the school's website.

○ Encourage students to get involved in activities outside of school. When possible, combine or coordinate with school and community organizations and clubs.

○ Include descriptions of teams, clubs, organizations, and other after-school activities in your student handbook. If your school has a website, list them there. Send handouts home to parents describing the various opportunities available to students.

○ Invite suggestions from students for new programs. Encourage kids to take leadership roles in creating and continuing these new groups.

○ Honor school staff members who volunteer with youth programs.

In the Community

○ Publicize youth programs in many different ways— through the media, posters, community bulletin boards, and websites. Often kids don't participate because they aren't aware that programs exist.

○ Use discounts, special promotional offers, and giveaways to attract young people to youth programs.

○ Make programs accessible. Try to locate them on bus lines and/or in neighborhoods where the kids are. Or offer transportation to and from.

○ Assess current programs—especially those that aren't attracting young people. Are they offering what young people *really* want and need, or what adults *think* they want and need?

○ Think intergenerationally. Start and support programs that connect old and young, adults and children.

○ Volunteer to lead or support a youth program in your neighborhood, community, or faith community.

○ Support school efforts to raise funds for extracurricular activities. Publish a "wish list" of equipment, supplies, and other wants and needs in the community newspaper and solicit donations.

○ Sponsor diverse activities to reach all kids and teens, especially those who are underserved by existing organizations.

○ Honor community members who volunteer with youth programs. Feature stories about them in local newspapers.

In the Faith Community

○ Coordinate youth program activities so they don't conflict with important extracurricular activities. *Example:* If many members of your youth group play baseball in the spring, try to work around their practice and game schedules.

○ Encourage young people to get involved in community groups, both as participants and as leaders.

✪ Encourage adult members to volunteer as sponsors for extracurricular activities.

✪ Regularly contribute to community youth organizations.

✪ Offer to sponsor an organization or club for young people, or give an existing organization a home. Many scout troops are sponsored by local faith communities.

ASSET #19
Religious Community

Kids spend one hour or more each week in religious services or participating in a faith community.

51% of the kids we surveyed have this asset in their lives.

At Home

○ Choose a faith community thoughtfully. When you find one that emphasizes your family's values, your children are more likely to internalize those values and make responsible decisions.

○ As much as possible, allow your kids to share in the choice about where to attend religious services. Or, if more than one service is offered, perhaps they could choose the time.

○ Encourage active involvement in religious activities by modeling active involvement. Don't just drop your kids off for services or classes and pick them up later.

○ Incorporate faith and spirituality into your daily life. Choose ways that best fit with your values and traditions.

○ When making important family decisions, consider them within the context of your faith.

✪ Volunteer to lead or assist with a religion class for young people.

At School

✪ Don't schedule school activities that conflict with important religious holidays, and be sure to consider the many different faith traditions within your school population (students, faculty, and staff).

✪ Communicate with local religious organizations. Share holiday and activity schedules. Try to coordinate with as many as possible to avoid major scheduling conflicts.

✪ If possible, incorporate information about religious holidays and traditions (across faiths) into class discussions. Be sure to check with your school policy first, since this is not permitted in some schools.

In the Community

✪ Don't schedule community activities that conflict with religious holidays, and be sure to consider the many different faith traditions within your community.

✪ Include youth leaders from faith communities on community-wide youth councils and task forces.

✪ Partner with local faith communities in sponsoring community-wide youth events.

✪ Sponsor a series of presentations on the different faiths in your community. Invite representatives from the various religious organizations to speak. Publicize the presentations.

○ Post faith community activities for young people on community websites and on local cable channels.

In the Faith Community

○ Develop strategies for your youth program that address the concerns, needs, interests, and issues of young people in your faith community.

○ Emphasize programming that keeps teens involved in the faith community throughout high school.

○ Include youth representation on your board.

○ Start a suggestion box for young people. Invite them to contribute their ideas for youth activities, programs, and special events.

○ Introduce a study group for young people and adults to learn more about your faith tradition. If desired, the group could also explore the history and practices of other faith traditions.

○ Don't lose touch with kids and teens over the summer. Maintain year-round connections and programs that will keep them interested and involved.

ASSET #20
Time at Home

Kids go out with friends "with nothing special to do" two or fewer nights each week.

56% of the kids we surveyed have this asset in their lives.

At Home

✪ Set limits on how often kids can go out with their friends during the school week. Have a family meeting to determine what seems reasonable and fair, starting with a basic guideline of four nights at home.

✪ Be firm about the four nights at home, but not inflexible. Encourage your children to get involved in creative activities, youth programs, and service to others. Make a distinction between having "something specific to do" and having "nothing special to do."

✪ Make time at home fun for everyone. Spend time together doing things you all enjoy. Play favorite games, have a family movie night, read, take walks, or go for bike rides.

✪ Be aware of where your children go and who they're with, even when they're teenagers.

✪ If your teenager has a part-time job, limit it to 15 hours or fewer a week during the school year. Studies have shown that teenagers who work more than 15 hours a week have more problems than those who work fewer hours.

✪ Allow your children to invite friends over on some (but not all) of their "at home" nights. *Examples:* Maybe the science study group could meet at your house, or your kids' friends could gather to watch a movie.

✪ Limit the amount of time your children spend at home alone. Plan to be home with them as much as you can. Sit down to dinner together. Be available to help with homework or just talk.

✪ Make your home a warm and inviting place for all family members—somewhere your kids *want* to be. If you feel that family members argue too much or have trouble communicating, seek outside help. Family counselors are experts in helping families get along better.

At School

✪ Limit the number of nights per week that students can be involved in school activities. Train adult leaders to help kids set priorities and limits.

✪ Encourage coaches, club sponsors, and others not to overschedule students.

✪ Spread special school events over the whole school year instead of grouping most of them around holidays or other occasions.

In the Community

- ✪ Limit the number of nights kids are expected to participate in activities.

- ✪ Create community calendars that include all different kinds of youth activities—in schools, faith communities, community organizations, parks, and other places. Distribute them widely (through a community newspaper, cable access, or a community website) so families can plan and set priorities together.

- ✪ Sponsor workshops for parents on communicating with kids. Offer suggestions for activities and projects families can do together.

- ✪ Limit the number of evenings adults are expected to participate in activities and meetings so they can spend more time at home with their children. Reinforce the importance of spending time at home.

In the Faith Community

- ✪ Encourage families to schedule regular "family nights." Offer suggestions for activities and projects to do as a family. Include ideas in worship bulletins and mailings to member households.

- ✪ Limit the number of evenings young people are expected to participate in activities related to your youth program.

- ✪ Limit the number of evenings adults are expected to participate in activities, meetings, classes, and committees so they can spend more time at home with their families.

ASSET BUILDING
IN ACTION

Like many countries in the world, South Africa grapples with a common problem: More and more children are becoming more and more sedentary, at the same time that many schools face budget cuts. Michael van Roodt of the Future Factory in Cape Town, saw that something needed to change. Children needed to get more exercise, and they also needed to build and strengthen their Developmental Assets. Van Roodt, along with other leaders in his sports development organization, visited schools to share the idea of creating asset-building sports programs.

Through their youth programs, the Future Factory has gotten kids active playing sports such as volleyball, soccer, and basketball. In addition, leaders teach kids traditional South African games and sports, such as kennetjie, drie blikkies, morabaraba, jukskei, kgati, and five stones.

The entire program was founded on asset building. Calling themselves the Asset Team, program leaders teach and reinforce the asset framework as part of their sports and recreation program. Future Factory leaders have received lots of positive feedback for their asset-building sports. Observers have described the program as "a life-changing experience for learners." Others report that kids have a newfound interest in school, and that the coaches' enthusiasm has been inspirational and contagious.

Tips for Teens
Build Your Own Assets

Asset #17: Creative Activities

GOAL: *To spend three or more hours per week in lessons or practice in music, theater, or other arts*

Participating in the arts—*any* of the arts—is a great way to develop your creativity, make new friends, master new skills, boost your brain power, and strengthen your self-esteem. Plus it's challenging, stimulating, rewarding, and fun. It feels good to be around art, and it feels even better to *make* art.

If your school offers classes, clubs, and after-school programs in music or the arts, you're lucky; many schools don't. Take advantage of these opportunities while they're available to you. If you'd love to play the cello but you can't afford to buy one, tell your teacher. Schools with music programs often have instruments available to borrow or rent. If that's not an option, ask for donations from community groups. Contact local newspapers and ask them to write stories about your school's search for musical instruments . . . or art supplies, lighting equipment for the drama club, a music system for the dance club, or whatever else you need.

Check with community education and arts organizations to see what's available there. You may find free or low-cost courses in calligraphy, photography, drawing, tap dance, singing, or playing the violin. Do your parents have talented friends? Maybe they can give you lessons in their specialties.

If your parents offer to pay for lessons, say yes . . . unless your dreams for yourself are different from the dreams they have for you. *Example:* They want you to play classical piano; you want to play jazz trumpet. Talk with them about your dreams. Ask for their help and support. You might propose a compromise: If they'll pay for this year's trumpet lessons, you'll try piano next year.

Keep in mind that it's less important to become a great performer (or painter, or writer) than it is to enjoy and appreciate what you do.

Asset #18: Youth Programs

GOAL: *To spend three or more hours per week in sports, clubs, or organizations at school and/or in the community*

If you're not thrilled by any of the teams, clubs, or organizations offered at your school, are you sure that you've checked into all of them? If you look again, you may find a special interest group you enjoy. If not, think about starting one. Find five to ten other students who share your interest, then get together and talk about the kind of group you'd like to start. Once you've defined your purpose, decided on a few goals, and outlined some possible activities, approach a teacher you like and ask him or her to sponsor your group.

Try looking beyond school, too. Learn what's available for kids your age at your community center, local arts organization, and faith community. Find out what civic groups offer. You'll probably discover groups especially for young people, as well as groups of adults that welcome young people. If you don't see anything that interests you, post messages on bulletin boards. You'll find other people who share your interests, and you can decide together what to do next.

Asset #19: Religious Community

GOAL: *To spend one hour or more per week in religious services or participating in a faith community*

Your faith community can be a source of support, encouragement, and affirmation throughout your life. A faith community of caring people who share similar values and views can be a good place to find adults to talk to—just what you need to build Asset #3 (Other Adult Relationships).

Many kids drop out of their faith communities as teenagers. Often, organized religion no longer seems relevant to their lives. Their parents may want them to keep attending services, but eventually decide that it's not worth arguing about. If you feel that your faith community is out of touch with young people, don't drop out. Speak up. Talk with the people who lead the youth program. Come with ideas and offer to help. Suggest a roundtable discussion—an opportunity for young people to express their opinions, thoughts, and needs.

Don't just expect your faith community to serve you. What can you contribute? *Example:* If you'd like your place of worship to offer one service a month especially for young people, maybe you could help organize it. The more involved you become, the more meaningful the experience will be for you, and the less likely you are to walk away.

If your parents aren't involved in a faith community, this doesn't mean that you can't be. Perhaps you can join a friend's, or visit the faith communities in your neighborhood or nearby. Talk with the people who lead the youth programs and explain that you're looking for a faith community to join.

What if your parents *are* involved in a faith community, but their choice doesn't seem right for you? Try talking with them about the way you feel. Maybe they will agree to help you find a community that better meets your spiritual needs.

Asset #20: Time at Home

GOAL: *To spend two or fewer nights each week out with friends "with nothing special to do"*

If your parents don't limit the amount of time you can spend away from home, try setting your own limits. Focus more on your schoolwork and your family, and see if your life changes in positive ways.

For young people with jobs, spending time at home often seems less important than putting in the hours at work. But consider this: when researchers at a university in Pennsylvania studied 1,800 high school students, they learned that those who worked more than 15 hours a week had more problems than those who worked fewer hours. Their schoolwork suffered. Their grades fell. They didn't score as well on achievement tests.

You may not have a choice; you may have to work more than 15 hours a week to help support your family. In this case, you're doing the best you can under the circumstances. But if you *do* have a choice, keep your hours to a minimum.

BUILDING INTERNAL ASSETS

COMMITMENT to LEARNING

Young people need to develop a lifelong commitment to education and learning.

The five **commitment to learning assets** are:

21. Achievement Motivation

22. School Engagement

23. Homework

24. Bonding to School

25. Reading for Pleasure

The more committed to learning a young person is, the more likely it is that he or she will grow up healthy.

ASSET #21
Achievement Motivation
Kids are motivated to do well in school.

71% of the kids we surveyed have this asset in their lives.

At Home

○ Clearly communicate to your children that you value learning—that you think school is important, and you want and expect them to take it seriously.

○ Model lifelong learning. Show an ongoing interest in learning new things, making new discoveries, and exploring new topics.

○ Stay in contact with teachers about your children's progress in school. Don't wait for report cards.

○ Encourage motivation *from the inside out.* Tap into your child's interests and passions, and try to connect them to what he or she is learning in school. Don't "pay" your child to learn with money, rewards, or excessive praise; that's motivation *from the outside in.*

○ Learn along with your children. Go someplace new together and explore. Read the same books and discuss them afterward, or take turns choosing books for everyone in the family to read. Take a community education class together. Brainstorm a list of questions you're all curious about, then visit the library to find the answers.

✪ Encourage your kids to do their best at school, but don't expect perfection. Leave room for mistakes.

✪ Relate what your child is learning in school to real-life situations. *Example:* Visit the capital city of your state when your child is studying state capitals.

✪ If your kids seem apathetic about school or resist going to school, try to find out why. Is school too easy for them, or too hard? Are they getting the help and support they need? Do they feel safe at school? Talk with their teachers. Do what you can to change things, working with other parents and school staff—or, if necessary and possible, switch schools.

At School

✪ Relate lesson content and curricula to real-life situations and issues. Use enrichment materials.

✪ People learn in different ways. Train teachers to recognize and teach to various learning styles, and to value the many different kinds of intelligence.

✪ Affirm and encourage achievement in diverse areas as students discover their own interests and capabilities.

✪ Encourage teachers to get to know their students. Personal attention and interest from a teacher can be powerful motivators.

✪ Check in with students periodically to make sure they're properly challenged and supported in their learning. If they aren't, discuss how you can work together to improve their experience.

✪ Honor and affirm students who do well in school. Award academic letters—like athletic letters—in official ceremonies. Feature star learners on bulletin boards along with star athletes. Encourage the local media to report on your community's academic achievers.

In the Community

✪ Make sure that your youth programming is enjoyable, meaningful, and intellectually challenging. Sponsor trips to museums, exhibits, films, lectures, and other learning opportunities.

✪ Encourage young people to use what they're learning in school to address issues in your youth program. For example, if they have been studying cultural diversity, they might have good suggestions for making your program more inclusive.

✪ Put motivated, achieving high school students together with younger kids on community projects. The older kids might inspire the younger ones.

✪ Start a Speakers' Bureau of high achievers in your community—including both adults and students. Publicize their availability to speak at area schools.

✪ Volunteer to be a tutor or a mentor in a school. Show that you value learning by donating your own time and expertise.

In the Faith Community

○ Affirm the value of education in all youth programming. Even if you disagree with the way a particular subject is taught, address that subject only; don't undermine education as a whole.

○ Make school a regular topic of conversation in youth groups.

○ Make youth programming intellectually challenging. Help young people see, appreciate, and think about the complexities in faith, theology, and ethics. Affirm kids who ask tough questions. When appropriate, have them apply skills they learn in school to the content of your youth program.

ASSET #22
School Engagement
Kids are actively engaged in learning.

62% of the kids we surveyed have this asset in their lives.

At Home

○ Talk with your children about school and learning. Ask them every day what they did in school, what they learned, what they liked about school, and what they didn't like about it. Stay in touch with their school experience.

○ Make learning a family affair. Learn more together about your children's favorite subjects. Involve them in your hobbies and interests. Learn a new skill together.

○ Help your children stay alert in school by ensuring that they eat well and get enough sleep.

○ Make it a point to attend school conferences and special events.

○ Help your kids explore all the options available at their school. They may not be aware of interesting opportunities.

○ Provide a positive learning environment in your home. Limit TV-watching time and time spent on the computer and/or cell phone. Have books, magazines, and newspapers available; eat dinner as a family and discuss current events.

○ Take it seriously when your child expresses boredom or frustration with school or mentions other problems (even small ones). Talk with the teachers right away.

○ Model lifelong learning. Take classes in your own areas of interest and talk to your kids about them.

At School

○ Conduct an "Interest Survey" at the start of the school year to find out what your students are interested in. Give them opportunities throughout the year to work on projects related to their interests.

○ Actively engage your students with a variety of teaching methods. Appeal to all of their senses; teach to every learning style.

○ Tie classroom learning to students' real-life situations, issues, and concerns. Draw connections between what they're learning in school and what's happening in their lives, in the community, and in the world; invite them to do the same.

○ Start an after-school or lunchtime discussion group where students can talk about issues, concerns, problems, fears, hopes, and dreams.

○ Ask students to evaluate their own learning experiences. Ask what they need to feel more engaged in and excited about school.

○ Make your classroom a warm and welcoming place to be.

○ Honor or reward teachers who are particularly effective in keeping students engaged in learning. Have students nominate and vote for a "Teacher of the Year."

In the Community

○ Ask kids and teens you meet and talk with how they're doing in school. Encourage them to do well. Talk positively about your own school experiences.

○ Work with the schools to develop lesson plans and curricula that relate to your community. *Example:* Is your town working to save a local stream? Preserve a historic site? Build a new library? Lessons related to these topics can link learning to real life.

○ Offer community education classes for the whole family.

○ Volunteer in a school as a tutor, club leader, or reader to young students, or in another helping role.

○ If your business employs young people, show genuine interest in their school performance. Encourage them to do well in school. Limit their work hours to no more than 15 per week—fewer during finals.

○ Sponsor an "Independent Study" program in cooperation with your local library. Encourage kids and adults to choose topics that interest them and to devote at least an hour each week to studying them individually. After a couple of months, participants could write brief reports about what they learned and share them through a community newsletter or website.

○ Counter messages in the media that describe school as meaningless or boring.

In the Faith Community

✪ Tie activities in the faith community to topics young people are studying in school.

✪ Survey young people about which topics they would like to learn more about. Invite experts in to teach and talk.

✪ Use a variety of learning and teaching methods in religious education settings. Ask the teachers in your faith community for ideas and suggestions. Learn about different learning styles.

✪ Be a learning faith community. Invite all members to discuss sacred writings; form intergenerational groups to discuss specific topics; visit local art museums to view religious paintings and sculpture.

ASSET #23
Homework

Kids do at least one hour of homework every school day.

53% of the kids we surveyed have this asset in their lives.

At Home

✪ Provide a quiet, comfortable, well-lit place for your kids to study without distractions. Together with your child, set boundaries about interruptions such as phone calls and visitors.

✪ Work with your child to set up a regular homework schedule, then respect it. Arrange dinner and family events around the homework schedule.

✪ Start a home reference library and keep it current. Begin with the basics: dictionary, thesaurus, almanac, desk encyclopedia, atlas. Add reference books on specific topics of interest to your child.

✪ If you have a home computer, consider purchasing an encyclopedia on CD-ROM; these are very affordable, especially when compared with traditional sets of encyclopedias. An Internet connection gives your kids access to vast amounts of reference materials and homework help. It also offers potential temptations and pitfalls. Talk with your child about differentiating between reliable and unreliable sources and about Internet safety.

○ Turn off the television and the computer and limit the hours your teen can spend at an after-school job. *Tip:* Experts recommend no more than 15 hours per week.

○ If homework time comes before dinner, make healthy snacks available. Hungry kids have trouble concentrating.

○ Be available to answer questions, do vocabulary drills, check homework, and offer support. Or study together; while your child does schoolwork, read, study something new, or catch up with some work.

○ Help your child prioritize homework assignments. (It's best to do the hard ones first—to get them out of the way before fatigue sets in.) Work with your child to plan long-term assignments.

○ Monitor homework. Don't hover, but do check in with your child every so often and ask "How's it going?"

At School

○ Regularly assign homework and hold students accountable for completing it and turning it in.

○ Communicate with other teachers about homework, test schedules, and long-term assignments. Spread them out evenly over the year so students aren't swamped.

○ Make homework relevant to other parts of students' lives— family, work, hobbies, community.

✪ Set up a homework hotline staffed by teachers, other adults, and older students. Start an online bulletin board or homework help chat room.

✪ Teach students how to use the library and the Internet to find reference materials and homework help.

In the Community

✪ Arrange after-school study programs. Set aside a quiet room for kids to do their homework, read, write, and study for tests. Staff it with adult mentors and tutors from the community.

✪ Expect young people to complete their homework as a requirement for participating in activities and programs. You won't be able to monitor this, but you can ask kids if they are keeping up with their homework and encourage them to do so. If enough adults express interest and concern, this becomes a community standard.

✪ Schedule a "homework hour" before after-school or evening activities.

✪ Publicize the resources of your public library and let kids know what kind of homework help they can find there.

✪ Set up a homework hotline staffed by volunteers from the community. Encourage the local high school to adopt this as a service project; give students service credits for working the hotline on school nights and weekends. Provide resources: telephones, desks and tables, dictionaries, computers, reference works (including, if possible, current editions of encyclopedias on CD-ROM), and an Internet connection.

In the Faith Community

⊙ Reduce conflicts between time commitments for faith community activities and homework. Try not to overschedule youth group members during the school year. Plan weeknight activities for later in the evening, after homework is finished.

⊙ Set up a homework hotline staffed by adults and high school students from the faith community.

⊙ Open the youth room after school as a study and homework center. Staff it with adult volunteers.

ASSET #24
Bonding to School

Kids care about their school.

61% of the kids we surveyed have this asset in their lives.

At Home

○ Kids can more easily bond to school when they know someone there cares about them. Tell your child about one adult and one peer in your school who cared about you. Ask your child which adult and which friends he or she likes best at school and why.

○ Encourage your child to participate in activities that boost school spirit.

○ Set up a school bulletin board in a prominent place in your home. Post the school calendar and school notices. Meet once a month to choose which school activities to attend as a family.

○ Encourage school pride by buying T-shirts, sweatshirts, caps, or other clothing with the school's name or logo for your child to wear. Display a school bumper sticker or window sticker on the family car.

○ Find out if the school newspaper is available online, or see if you can subscribe through the mail. Read it and discuss it with your child.

○ Invite a teacher to go out for breakfast, lunch, or coffee with you and your child. Invite a teacher to dinner at your home.

○ Write thank-you notes, leave voicemail messages, or send email to teachers and administrators when you're pleased about something at your child's school.

○ Listen to your children when they complain about school or talk about not feeling connected to school. Is there a specific problem that should be addressed? Take any concerns to your child's teachers. Be calm and respectful.

○ Show that *you* care about your child's school. Join a parent-teacher organization; attend school conferences and special events; volunteer as a tutor, club advisor, or parent helper.

At School

○ Provide many opportunities for students to celebrate and boost school spirit. *Examples:* Have a schoolwide contest to choose a new school slogan, T-shirt motif, song, or cheer. Decorate bulletin boards and walls with school spirit slogans and symbols. Have each classroom or homeroom design its own banner. Give monthly "School Spirit Awards" to the most caring, enthusiastic, and involved students, teachers, administrators, support staff members, and volunteers.

○ Produce school T-shirts, sweatshirts, caps, jackets, buttons, and other items so students can wear visible signs of their school affiliation.

❂ Provide many opportunities for parents (and other adults) to volunteer at school. Volunteering encourages parents to care about their kids' school, and their enthusiasm gets passed along to their children.

❂ Make sports, arts, drama, band, choir, and other school programs inclusive so all kids can participate.

❂ Create a school publication open to all students. Invite them to contribute columns, interviews, creative writing, art, photographs, or cartoons.

❂ Invite alumni to write articles for the school newspaper, yearbook, or website about what the school means to them.

❂ Don't limit school spirit to one type of activity (typically sports). Celebrate many strengths in your school.

In the Community

❂ Support school fund-raising efforts (*examples:* bond issues, candy sales), read-athons, and teams.

❂ Attend school performances, plays, and concerts.

❂ Recognize entire schools or classrooms. Reward students for good attendance.

❂ Highlight school accomplishments in the local media, at civic gatherings, and anywhere else you can think of.

❂ Have students share their school experiences with community leaders and groups.

❂ Never allow the quality of schools to suffer because of a lack of financial resources.

In the Faith Community

✪ Give young people opportunities to talk about their school experiences. Your faith community might include kids from many area schools. Sharing can help them connect with each other and also communicate pride in their schools.

✪ As your community is able, support young people who are fund-raising for their schools.

✪ Encourage adult members to attend school activities involving young people from your faith community. Announce them in the bulletin or newsletter.

ASSET #25
Reading for Pleasure

Kids read for pleasure three or more hours per week.

23% of the kids we surveyed have this asset in their lives.

At Home

✪ Model reading for pleasure. Talk with your children about what you're reading; make your enthusiasm for reading obvious to them. Explain how reading gives you pleasure while helping you learn about life and the world.

✪ Set aside a regular family reading time each day or week.

✪ Make reading aloud a family activity. Read to your kids as long as they'll let you. When they're old enough, take turns reading out loud to each other.

✪ Give your kids access to many different types of reading material: books, newspapers, encyclopedias, almanacs, magazines. Give books and magazine subscriptions for birthdays and holidays. Put bookcases in your children's rooms so they can fill them with their favorite books.

✪ Pay regular visits to the library. Children who are old enough to write their names should have their own library cards.

- Limit television watching and time spent on the Internet.
- Read the same books as a family and talk about them afterward. Let your children choose some of the books your family reads.
- Play word games such as Scrabble and Boggle together. Put magnetic words and letters on the refrigerator and write messages and poems to each other.
- When a movie based on a book is released (and it's something your family wants to see), read the book first. Then go to the movie together or rent it to watch at home. Afterward, talk about how the two compare.

At School

- Provide quiet time during the school day for students to read—and a cozy corner of the classroom where they can go. Let them choose what they want to read.
- Make many types of books available in the classroom—fact-filled almanacs, books of quotations, storybooks, picture books, reference books, and more.
- If some kids don't like to read or have difficulty reading, let them listen to audiobooks.
- Have students write book reviews for the school newspaper or website. They might also give brief reviews over the morning announcements or your school's closed-circuit TV network.
- Feature fun books in the library. Form a student committee to read and recommend books.

✪ Start an after-school book club. Be sure to choose a wide range of books to read so that many different types of readers are interested and feel comfortable participating.

✪ Pair younger students with older students who love to read.

✪ Help students write their own books; start a classroom library of student-created books.

In the Community

✪ Emphasize the importance of reading by volunteering to read to kids at schools, libraries, community centers, recreation centers, and parks.

✪ Have a community-wide read-athon. Reward students who participate with a congratulatory letter from the mayor or a local celebrity.

✪ Donate quality books and audiobooks to schools, libraries, bookmobiles, childcare centers, and other places young people spend time.

✪ Make sure your local libraries are adequately funded and staffed. Keep them open after school and on weekends.

✪ Encourage bookstores to feature great books for young people.

✪ Start "Frequent Reader Clubs" for kids of all ages, with incentives for participating. Promote the clubs with posters and flyers in area businesses and places where kids hang out.

✪ Have a community-wide drive to gather used books, then donate them to needy families and/or shelters.

In the Faith Community

✪ Create a library and reading room for young people in your faith community. Keep it stocked with all kinds of books that might interest them (ask for their suggestions).

✪ Include current books for kids in the faith community's library.

✪ Have kids and teens serve as readers during services.

✪ Refer to books in sermons and religious education classes.

✪ Invite kids to write book reviews for the newsletter on books that relate to issues or concerns in the faith community.

ASSET BUILDING
IN ACTION

In San Jose, California, Linda Silvius works with Project Cornerstone, a group devoted to building communities and schools in which adults help young people thrive. "Parents are our army in this asset-building movement," says Silvius. "Asset building has given parents a voice."

Silvius met with parents to talk about assets, goals, and ideas. From those discussions grew activities supporting a commitment to learning. For example:

▶ One parent, whose first grader was being bullied, met with the principal and said she wanted to create a school reading program to decrease bullying and increase friendship skills between children. She started ABC Parents (Asset-Building Champion Parents). Now 120 parents read to more than 5,000 students every month.

▶ At Booksin Elementary School, parent volunteers help out at school every Friday, reading to kids and playing with them during lunch and recess.

▶ Spanish-speaking moms read bilingual books to kids at school. "These parents used to come and not say anything," Silvius said. "Now they're the leaders."

Steps like these have improved school climate. Silvius says, "We're changing the world one kid, one mom, one dad, and one teacher at a time."

Tips for Teens
Build Your Own Assets

Asset #21: Achievement Motivation

GOAL: *To be motivated to do well in school*

Do you sometimes feel as if school is a waste of your time? You can do something about it. Take charge of your education. Set goals for yourself, ask questions in class, and find an ally—a teacher or school counselor who can help you get the most out of school.

Consider your friends' attitudes toward school. If you're spending most of your time with kids who hate school and do the minimum work needed to pass, maybe you need a wider range of friends.

School success is an important step toward getting a good job, college or trade school admission, scholarships, financial aid, and other aspects of becoming independent and achieving your goals. If your grades could use some boosting, see what's available at your school. Can you get a tutor to help you with some subjects? Can you ask your teachers for tips on raising your grades?

Often, grades are a combination of factors: assignments done, papers turned in on time, test scores, class participation. Don't make the mistake of skipping assignments or turning papers in a day late. What seems to you like an insignificant little worksheet can affect your final grade.

Asset #22: School Engagement

GOAL: *To be actively engaged in learning*

You'll spend 13 years of your life in school—longer if you continue your education in college, trade school, and/or graduate school. You can view school as a prison sentence or an adventure; it's up to you. Your teachers can try to inspire you; your parents can try to encourage you; but what you get out of school depends on *your* attitude, *your* enthusiasm, *your* willingness to learn.

If you're already excited about school, that's great. If you're not, how can you get excited? What can you do to make learning more interesting and enjoyable? Even in the dullest, deadliest class, you can probably find *one* thing that sparks your interest. Pursue it. Try to relate what you're learning to real life. Tell your teachers (and your parents) that you want to become more engaged in your own learning. Ask for their support and suggestions. Make the effort to stay awake and alert in class (*tip:* sit up front, if possible) and keep up with the assignments. Ask questions if there's something you don't understand. Participate in class discussions. Deepen your understanding of a subject by doing a special project or interviewing an expert. Investigate something you're curious about. Come up with your own ideas for getting involved in your education—and try them out. You have nothing to lose and much to gain.

Asset #23: Homework

GOAL: *To do at least one hour of homework every school day*

Make homework your first priority—before texting, email, TV, time with your friends, extracurricular activities, even a job. What if you don't have at least five hours of homework in a typical week? Spend the time reading more about a particular subject, practicing your skills, or reviewing your books and notes. It's important to form the homework habit *now,* especially if you plan to go to college.

If you have a part-time job during the school year, limit your work schedule to 15 or fewer hours per week to allow time for homework and other activities that are important to your overall development.

Asset #24: Bonding to School

GOAL: *To care about your school*

If you're feeling disconnected from your school—tuned-out, bored, uninterested, as if it's just a place you have to go—talk to a parent, teacher, school counselor, or other adult. Work together to identify ways you can feel more connected.

You might start by identifying one program or activity that you really like about your school, and then getting involved with it. Or identify one thing you especially love to do, and find out if your school offers anything—a course, a club, a team—that matches your interest. If you don't find anything that sparks your interest, start something yourself. Find an adult sponsor (usually a teacher) who's willing to support you. Write a proposal for your club and present it to the principal, faculty, or club coordinator at your school. Then advertise your club to attract new members.

Brainstorm ways to boost school spirit in yourself and other students. What about having a schoolwide contest to design a school symbol or create a school slogan? Could your group or club create inspiring banners for the halls? Are there good things happening at your school that the community should know about? Maybe you could write news releases for the media or help maintain your school's website.

If your school has serious school spirit problems—if most students seem disconnected or apathetic—find a school in your community where school spirit is strong. Learn what they're doing differently. Talk with teachers, administrators, and student leaders. Bring some of their ideas back to your school.

Asset #25: Reading for Pleasure

GOAL: *To spend three or more hours per week reading for pleasure*

Don't underestimate the importance of reading. It's vital to your current and future success. The more you read, the stronger your reading skills will become. Skilled readers perform better on tests, read more quickly and easily, and get more out of what they read. They're more likely to ask questions when they don't understand something; to look up words they don't know; and to take notes on what they read.

If you haven't yet formed the reading-for-pleasure habit, it's not too late. Think of something—anything—you'd like to know more about, then visit the library. Ask the librarian to help you find a book or magazine on that topic. Once you've read that, read another. Or search the Internet for articles that interest you. Three hours per week of reading may sound like a lot, but it's less than 26 minutes a day. (So skip a TV show, or spend a little less time online.)

To give yourself and your friends an extra push toward reading for pleasure, consider starting a book club. Decide each month on a book you'd all like to read and set a deadline for reading it. Afterward, get together and talk about it.

POSITIVE VALUES

Young people need to develop strong values that guide their choices.

The six **positive values assets** are:

26. Caring

27. Equality and Social Justice

28. Integrity

29. Honesty

30. Responsibility

31. Restraint

The more a young person develops positive values that guide her or his behavior, the more likely it is that she or he will make positive choices and grow up healthy.

ASSET #26
Caring

Kids place high value on helping other people.

52% of the kids we surveyed have this asset in their lives.

At Home

○ Regularly spend family time helping others. Volunteer at your local food shelf, at shelters or soup kitchens for homeless people, at eldercare facilities. It's tremendously inspiring for kids to see their parents helping others and to know that they can make a difference, too.

○ Show care and concern for your neighbors. Is there an elderly person who needs help with shopping and home maintenance? Someone who could use a hand with yard work? Set a good example and get your kids involved.

○ Have family meetings to brainstorm ways of helping people. Decide together that you'll spend a certain number of hours each week serving others.

○ Instead of spending money on holiday gifts for each other, identify a family in need. (Ask at your child's school, at your community center, and/or at your place of worship.) Then work together as a family to compile a list of gifts and necessities and shop for them. Arrange to have everything delivered anonymously.

○ Establish an atmosphere of mutual caring and helpfulness within your home.

○ Encourage your teen to help other people and support his or her efforts, even in some cases when it feels uncomfortable. For example, it may seem risky to do a cleanup project in a high-crime neighborhood, but as long as appropriate precautions are taken, the benefits for everyone can far outweigh the risks.

At School

○ Encourage all students to participate in service activities or service-learning classes. Give credits, not grades, for participation. Work with your community to learn where students can be of the most service, then offer a range of options.

○ Provide cooperative learning opportunities for all students. The brightest students shouldn't always be the ones who are helping others. Work with your less able students to identify their special talents and abilities so they can be helpers, too.

○ Create a peer counseling program in your school. Train students to guide their peers in resolving conflicts and making good decisions.

○ Honor and affirm students who help others. Give special awards and recognition for service.

○ Honor and affirm school staff who are active in community service. Promote them as role models. Start a mentoring program to match students with caring staff.

✪ Study people from the past and present who are good examples of caring. Discuss their contributions to the world.

In the Community

✪ Include service projects and reflection on these experiences as an integral part of all youth programming.

✪ Work closely with your community to identify opportunities for young people to serve others. Invite young people to brainstorm service ideas.

✪ Honor and affirm kids and teens who serve others. Sponsor an annual awards program and publicize it in the local media.

✪ Identify community members who are active in serving others. Invite them to speak to young people. Encourage them to mentor young people who want to serve.

✪ Participate in neighborhood rehabilitation projects. Encourage community members and their kids to help.

✪ Form relationships with national service organizations. Invite representatives to speak in your community. Encourage community members—kids and adults—to volunteer with the organizations of their choice.

✪ Teach young people caring skills and provide ample opportunities to use them within the community.

In the Faith Community

⚙ Make young people aware of the service opportunities available within your faith community. Announce them during worship services. Provide opportunities for kids and adults to serve together.

⚙ Include peer helping in your youth programming.

⚙ Make young people aware of service opportunities beyond the faith community.

⚙ Invite kids and teens to contribute their own ideas for helping others.

⚙ Honor and affirm members of all ages who help others.

ASSET #27
Equality and Social Justice

Kids place high value on promoting equality and reducing hunger and poverty.

54% of the kids we surveyed have this asset in their lives.

At Home

○ As a family, discuss your views about equality and social justice. Choose a cause to follow and help.

○ Gather information about organizations that assist or advocate for people who are poor, hungry, or suffering from inequalities. Have a family discussion to decide which one(s) your family will support. Young children can set aside part of their allowance; older kids can chip in a portion of their earnings from jobs and chores.

○ Instead of spending money on holiday gifts, make a family contribution to a charitable organization or other worthy cause.

○ Volunteer with your family at a soup kitchen, homeless shelter, or food pantry. Join marches and demonstrations for equality and social justice.

○ Talk with your children about world disasters and countries where people are suffering. Watch news programs, read newspapers, visit the library, and search the Internet for more information. Is there something that especially touches your children, or affects them in some way? A war, famine, an earthquake, a fire, or a flood? Find a way for your family to help. *Tip:* Newspapers often publish the names, addresses, and telephone numbers of relief organizations following major disasters, and television news programs announce them or scroll them at the bottom of the screen.

○ Take family vacations in which you expose your kids firsthand to communities in need. *Example:* If you visit Washington, D.C., don't just focus on the famous and exciting tourist sites. Also learn about areas of the city with serious problems.

○ Visit museums that address issues of equality and social justice.

At School

○ Include equality and social justice as ongoing topics in class discussions and curricula. Assign research projects on current issues and events.

○ Invite representatives from national and international service, relief, and human rights organizations to speak to students. If possible, have small group discussions so students and adults can interact one-on-one.

○ Offer a unit of study on people who have made a difference in the world through activism and service.

✪ Sponsor schoolwide emphases on particular issues and concerns, then address them in all areas of the curriculum.

In the Community

✪ Work in cooperation with the school district, scouts, or other organizations on a food drive, clothing drive, or other project that promotes equality and social justice. Encourage students to be on your city's Human Rights Commission.

✪ Give young people responsibility and leadership for service projects. Let them prove to themselves that they can make a difference.

✪ Sponsor community discussions about equality and social justice. Invite representatives from service and relief organizations to speak. Schedule the discussions for a time when kids can attend with their parents.

✪ Post fact sheets about hunger, poverty, inequality, and injustice on bulletin boards. Have brochures available from service and relief organizations.

✪ Research charities and nonprofits and post a list of reliable, well-respected organizations on a community website or in a newsletter.

✪ Always take time to talk with young people after they have completed service projects. This helps them understand the issues and make important connections between their actions and how they affect others.

In the Faith Community

✪ Address issues of equality and social justice in your youth programming. Sponsor discussions and arrange ways for young people to get involved.

✪ Address these issues in sermons, homilies, and messages to the faith community.

✪ Invite young people to contribute their ideas when planning ways for your faith community to address global concerns.

✪ Through trips, speakers, service projects, and simulations, make world issues personally relevant to young people.

✪ Honor and affirm members who volunteer or work for service and relief organizations.

ASSET #28
Integrity

*Kids act on their convictions
and stand up for their beliefs.*

71% of the kids we surveyed have this asset in their lives.

At Home

○ Model integrity in your daily life. Talk openly about what you believe and value, then act on what you say. When it comes to building positive values, *you* are your child's most important teacher.

○ Have a family discussion about the meaning of integrity. Define it as simply as you can. *Examples:* being true to your convictions and beliefs; "talking the talk and walking the walk."

○ Ask your children to articulate their convictions and beliefs. What do they stand for? What's important to them? Come up with a list of convictions and beliefs that everyone in your family shares. Post it in your home.

○ Tell your child about a time when you stood up for something even though it was difficult to do. Explain how you felt. Then tell your child about a time when you *didn't* stand up for something because you were afraid. Discuss why it's easier to act on your convictions in some situations than others.

- Gently but firmly call your children's attention to times when their words and actions don't match. Encourage them to do the same for you.

- Celebrate when your child acts on a belief or conviction, especially when it was obviously hard to do.

- Whenever you notice or learn about someone who acts with integrity, point it out to your children.

- Comment on people's actions in the news and how they show (or don't show) integrity.

- Share with your children times when you're tempted to ignore your values and beliefs. *Example:* "Today a clerk gave me change for a 50 instead of a 5. I could have used the extra money, but I gave it back."

- Affirm and support your children when they make choices that show integrity—even if they aren't the choices you'd make.

At School

- Include integrity in your school's stated and posted values and expectations. Look for ways to explore what it means with students of all ages.

- Encourage and expect all faculty and staff to model integrity.

- Ask students to tell in their own words what integrity means to them. Have them give examples of people who acted with integrity.

- Create an Integrity Bulletin Board and feature people who have acted with integrity. *Examples:* Gandhi, Martin Luther King Jr., Abraham Lincoln, Sojourner Truth. Invite students to nominate people they know for the bulletin board—including each other. They should be prepared to explain why they are nominating someone.

✪ Highlight men and women in history and current events who acted with integrity. Find examples in literature and discuss them as a class.

In the Community

✪ Model integrity in your daily life—at home, in the workplace, in public, and wherever you go. Support and affirm kids when they act with integrity.

✪ Launch a community-wide campaign on the value of integrity. Use billboards, posters, grocery bags, flyers, local media, and the Internet to spread the word.

✪ Sponsor speeches, seminars, presentations, and roundtable discussions on the topic of integrity. Be sure to include children and teens.

In the Faith Community

✪ Model integrity as individuals and as a faith community. Clearly articulate your values and beliefs and act on them.

✪ Talk about the importance of integrity within your faith tradition and sacred texts.

✪ Address integrity in sermons, homilies, worship bulletins, and mailings to member households. Give examples of people from your faith tradition (and your faith community) who have acted with integrity.

✪ Include integrity in your faith community's stated values and expectations. Make it a frequent topic in your youth programming.

ASSET #29
Honesty

Kids tell the truth, even when it's not easy.

69% of the kids we surveyed have this asset in their lives.

At Home

○ Model honesty in your daily life. Be honest with your children, your spouse, telemarketers, solicitors, store clerks, coworkers, friends, neighbors, relatives—and yourself.

○ Encourage and expect family members to be honest with themselves and each other. Honestly acknowledge feelings. Honestly admit to successes and mistakes.

○ "Catch" your children being honest.

○ When you fudge the truth, admit it and apologize.

○ Don't overreact when your child lies to you. Children will lie if they fear your reaction. If you suspect or know that your child is lying, ask "Do you think I believe you right now? Or do you think I might be having trouble believing you right now?" Give your child the opportunity to tell the truth.

○ Have family members discuss situations they observed at work, at school, and in the community where people acted honestly and dishonestly.

✪ Point out when characters in TV shows and movies are being honest or dishonest. Are there any consequences for dishonesty? Do the consequences seem real?

✪ Point out dishonesty in advertising.

✪ Talk with your kids about ways the Internet can encourage honesty and dishonesty.

✪ Help your children talk through situations in which it's tempting to be dishonest. Think of solutions together.

✪ Never punish your kids for being honest with you.

At School

✪ Include honesty in your school's stated and posted values and expectations.

✪ Establish clear boundaries and consequences for dishonest behavior (lying, cheating, stealing, plagiarism, false accusations). Publish them in the school handbook.

✪ Make it easier for students to be honest than to be dishonest.

✪ Teach honesty skills in the classroom. Have students role-play what to do and say when it's hard to tell the truth; when telling the truth might hurt someone's feelings; when they're caught telling a lie.

✪ Use case studies and simulations to highlight times when it's hard to be honest. Point out ways to be honest even then.

✪ Encourage and expect all faculty and staff to model honesty.

- Ask students to tell in their own words what honesty means to them. Have them give examples of people who acted honestly and dishonestly.
- Create a classroom display about honesty. Feature people in history who told the truth, inspiring quotations about honesty, books about honesty, and stories about honesty from newspapers, magazines, and websites.
- Work with students to write a Code of Honesty for your classroom or school.

In the Community

- Make honesty a community value. Hold public officials and local celebrities to high standards of honesty. Remind them that they are role models.
- Notice and affirm young people who act with honesty. *Examples:* the child who returns too much change at the store; the neighborhood kid who admits to sending a baseball through your window.
- Feature stories in the media about people who acted honestly.
- Be willing to get involved when you witness dishonest behavior.

In the Faith Community

- Model honesty as individuals and as a faith community. Be honest in your dealings with your membership, your neighbors, and your community.
- Make honesty the topic of sermons, homilies, articles in worship bulletins, and mailings to member households.

○ Use sacred writings and stories to illustrate the importance of honesty.

○ Give members a safe space to struggle with tough ethical and personal situations in which honesty can be difficult.

○ Encourage children and teens to commit to being honest together. (They might even sign an "honesty pledge" as a group.) This can be a source of strength and support when kids are pressured to cheat or be dishonest in other ways.

ASSET #30
Responsibility

Kids accept and take personal responsibility for their actions and decisions.

67% of the kids we surveyed have this asset in their lives.

At Home

○ Model responsibility in your daily life. When you make a commitment, follow through. When you can't or don't do something you should have, don't make excuses. Talk with your child about how you plan to avoid getting into a similar situation in the future.

○ Keep track of responsibilities with to-do lists. Encourage your kids to make lists of their own.

○ Create a family chores chart and list everyone's responsibilities.

○ Give your children opportunities to be responsible. Don't assume that a task is beyond their capabilities—but do keep your expectations realistic and allow for mistakes.

○ Break new tasks into smaller steps and teach them one by one until your child can take responsibility for the entire task alone.

✪ Make time to teach responsibility. Don't rush your children through new tasks; don't squeeze them in when you're in a hurry or pressured to be elsewhere or doing other things.

✪ Don't nag or rescue your kids when they "forget" to follow through on a responsibility. Let natural consequences occur. *Example:* Kids who don't put their dirty clothes in the laundry basket will run out of clean clothes to wear.

✪ Recognize and affirm your child's responsible behavior.

✪ Give kids more responsibility as they mature. Keep tasks and expectations age-appropriate. If you're not sure what's suitable for your child, ask an expert or read a book about child development. *Tip:* Other parents can be experts, too.

At School

✪ Expect students to act responsibly. Notice and affirm them when they do; set clear and reasonable consequences for when they don't.

✪ Give students real responsibilities within the classroom and the school. Monitor but don't take over.

✪ Teach students how to make and use to-do lists.

✪ Don't assume that students know how to tackle large assignments. Show them how to break a large assignment into smaller parts, figure out what they need to complete each part, and set deadlines for themselves. Have older students teach this to younger students.

✪ Follow through on your commitments to your students.

In the Community

○ Challenge assumptions that young people are naturally irresponsible. Call attention to ways that kids can and do act responsibly.

○ Make responsibility a community value. Hold community leaders to high standards. Expect them to take personal responsibility for their actions and decisions.

○ Implement a restorative justice program in your community. Don't just punish kids who break the law or violate community standards; insist that they take responsibility for their actions and repair any damage they have done.

○ Be clear and explicit about job responsibilities for teen workers and teach them how to meet those responsibilities.

In the Faith Community

○ Give kids real responsibilities within the faith community. Assign specific tasks to children and teens and expect them to follow through.

○ Make responsibility the topic of sermons, homilies, articles in worship bulletins, and mailings to member households.

○ Offer workshops, seminars, and discussion groups for parents on the topic of teaching kids to be responsible.

○ Support young people when they're in situations in which it's difficult to carry out their responsibilities.

ASSET #31
Restraint

Kids believe that it's important not to be sexually active or to use alcohol or other drugs.

47% of the kids we surveyed have this asset in their lives.

At Home

✪ Talk with your kids as openly as you can about sex, alcohol, and other drugs. If you're uncomfortable discussing certain topics, admit it and provide age-appropriate books. Encourage your kids to talk with other adults you (and they) know and trust.

✪ Be clear about your boundaries, values, and reasons. Many teenagers are actually *relieved* to hear their parents say "We expect you not to have sex or drink alcohol as a teenager." Explain why—and be open to questions.

✪ Invite your teenagers to make a commitment not to have sex or use alcohol during their teenage years. Many teens today are choosing to abstain, and some are going public with their decision. They're finding that this frees them from some of the pressures that other kids experience.

✪ With your teenager, take turns stating your opinions and values on issues such as one-night stands, drinking and driving, drugs, alcohol at parties, teen pregnancy, and so on.

○ Talk with your kids about the benefits of restraint, but also be honest about the challenges. Consider tactics for exercising restraint when it's difficult to do so.

○ Look for opportunities in the media (newspaper or magazine articles, TV programs, movies) to bring up the topics of sexual activity, alcohol, or drug use. Discuss your reaction and ask for your child's opinion. Be as straightforward and honest as you can.

○ If you learn that your teenagers are already sexually active or using alcohol or other drugs, encourage them to reconsider their choice in light of values that are important to them. *Example:* If they strongly believe in justice, talk about how having sex too early often exploits one person in the relationship. You might also seek professional guidance on how to respond appropriately.

○ Teach and model appropriate ways to show affection.

○ Model restraint. If you drink alcohol, use moderation. Never drink and drive.

○ Tell your children that if they ever find themselves in a situation in which others are pressuring them to have sex or get drunk or high, they can call you and you'll come to get them—no questions asked.

At School

○ Give students opportunities to express their values, attitudes, and concerns about sex, alcohol, and drugs. Start a lunchtime or after-school discussion group.

○ Stock the media center with appropriate resources (books, magazines, videos) on sex, alcohol, and drugs.

✪ Train peer counselors to affirm young people who choose abstinence.

✪ Work with students to create a school pledge about staying alcohol- and drug-free. Make copies available for students to sign, and inform the local media about this effort.

✪ If sex education is taught in your school, use a values-based curriculum that helps kids sort out their individual values and understand how those values shape their behaviors.

✪ Invite the mayor to speak at D.A.R.E. graduations. Send congratulatory letters to graduates.

In the Community

✪ Support local efforts to reduce or eliminate youth access to sexually explicit movies, videos, and magazines, as well as to alcohol and tobacco.

✪ Have clear expectations of how young people should relate to each other in all activities. Emphasize mutual respect and responsibility.

✪ Create a climate in which abstinence is valued and affirmed.

✪ Invite community health professionals to speak to parents and kids about sex, alcohol, and drugs.

In the Faith Community

✪ Include discussions about restraint in your faith community's educational programming. Clearly communicate what your faith tradition teaches about sexual behavior and the use of alcohol or drugs.

○ Find ways for young people to affirm and support each other in making positive choices about sex, alcohol, and drugs. Help them articulate the reasons for their decisions.

○ Invite young people to make a commitment not to have sex or use alcohol during their teenage years. If appropriate, they can do this publicly; if not, privately.

○ Even if teenagers have been sexually active, encourage and affirm decisions to stop. Talk with sexually active teens about important values they can build by refraining from sexual activity.

ASSET BUILDING
IN ACTION

A service learning project at Father Marquette Middle School in Marquette, Michigan, gave fifth-grade students exposure to bread making. It also gave them an up close experience with the positive values and Developmental Assets of caring and social justice.

Teacher Jill Koski's class baked bread twice a month and delivered it to residents of Janzen House, a local transition residence for homeless members of the community and others needing help.

Koski and her students came up with the idea. "The kids love it," Koski said. "Parents provide the recipes and the ingredients. The parents and I serve as the kids' helpers." The students worked in teams of four and learned about cooperation and management. They also got to apply math skills and explore some basic science principles.

But delivering the bread was the highlight. "We've been to Janzen House when the residents have been there, and the children have been humbled by the experience," said Koski.

Tips for Teens
Build Your Own Assets

Asset #26: Caring

GOAL: *To believe that it's really important to help other people*

There are many opportunities within your school, neighborhood, and community to reach out and help others. Countless young people have made (and are making) a difference in people's lives. Look around you for examples. You might have to look carefully, because children and teens who help others often don't make a big deal about it and might not get much recognition. Ask adults you know—teachers, youth group leaders, religious leaders—to point you toward kids who are making a difference. Talk with those kids and ask them why they do it. You'll probably hear that the more they give, the more they *get* in return—respect, self-esteem, self-worth, and the satisfaction that comes from having open hands and an open heart.

The next step is choosing a problem that you want to help solve. Find something that interests you on a personal level. Would you like to help homeless people? Hungry kids? A lonely neighbor? Abused or abandoned animals? Learn more about the problem, enlist friends to work with you, brainstorm ideas, and get started.

If you're not ready to tackle a big project, you can show that you care in simpler ways. Perform little acts of kindness for your family, friends, and classmates. Say something nice to or about another person. Leave a small gift or a thoughtful note in a friend's locker or on a teacher's desk. Or just smile at someone—a quick way to show you care. Decide to be a caring person and you'll discover that the possibilities are endless.

Asset #27: Equality and Social Justice

GOAL: *To help promote equality and reduce world poverty and hunger*

We are all citizens of the world. An ever-widening range of technology and ways to communicate instantaneously has made it possible to stay on top of news from almost everywhere around the globe. Turn on CNN, listen to public radio, read newspapers and magazines, or search the Internet to educate yourself about the world's people and problems. *Tip:* Check out the Human Rights Web (www.hrweb.org), a great online source of information about human rights issues.

You can't singlehandedly stop a war or save a nation, but you can do *something*. Help support a relief organization or human rights organization. (Amnesty International is the oldest and the biggest.) Join a letter-writing campaign. Get involved with your local chapter of Habitat for Humanity, an international organization that builds homes for families in need. Volunteer at a local service organization or through your faith community. Every effort, however small it may seem, has the potential to change someone else's life—and yours—profoundly.

Asset #28: Integrity

GOAL: *To be someone who acts on your convictions and stands up for your beliefs*

What do you stand for? What *won't* you stand for? Are you someone who acts on your convictions and beliefs? How do you know? One way to find out is by making a list of qualities that are important to you. Your list might include honesty, honor, trustworthiness, genuineness, and consistency. Do you have these qualities? If so, how can you strengthen them even further? If not, how can you build them in yourself?

You can start by finding an adult role model—someone you see as having integrity. This person "talks the talk and walks the walk." It might be a parent, a teacher, a neighbor, a religious leader, or another adult you know and trust. Spend time together; get to know him or her. Ask the person to tell you about times when acting on his or her convictions wasn't easy. Share your own concerns. *Examples:* How can you know when to speak up and when to stay silent? Is it always worth it to be assertive? Can having integrity ever get you into trouble? What happens when your convictions clash with your parents' convictions?

You can also visit the library and look for books about integrity, or do some investigation online. (Ask the librarian for help if you need it.) Read and think about the materials you find. If you're interested in exploring this topic with friends, read the same books or articles as a group and talk about them afterward.

Try to surround yourself with people of integrity—friends who act on their convictions and stand up for their beliefs. Then you can support each other during tough times.

Asset #29: Honesty

GOAL: *To tell the truth—even when it's not easy*

Surround yourself with friends who value honesty. These are people who don't lie about losing their homework when they just didn't do it; who don't tell their parents they're going one place when they're really going somewhere else; who don't spread gossip and rumors. Reinforce each other's efforts to be honest.

You can also make a personal commitment to tell the truth. Tell someone you trust about your commitment—a parent, teacher, close friend, youth group leader—and ask for support. Go to that person when being honest is especially difficult for you.

When you're honest, people trust you. Adults allow you more privileges and freedom. Friends know they can count on you. You gain a good reputation because most people admire and respect honesty. You get into less trouble and feel more secure and confident in yourself.

Asset #30: Responsibility

GOAL: *To accept and take personal responsibility for your actions and decisions*

You can accept and take more responsibility in all areas of your life. Start by brainstorming ways you can take more responsibility at home. Are there additional chores you could be doing? Other ways you could be helping? Could you take more responsibility for meeting your own needs? You might imagine what your life would be like if you were living on your own. Who would do your laundry? Prepare your meals? Clean your room? Manage your money? Make sure you got to school (or work) on time? How many of these tasks are your parents doing for you? How many could you do for yourself? *Tip:* Most parents notice and appreciate responsible behavior in their kids. And they tend to reward it with more privileges and freedom. It's a win-win situation.

Next, think of ways you can take more responsibility at school. Then focus on your community, your friends, and your personal goals. The more responsibility you take, the stronger and more capable you'll feel.

Asset #31: Restraint

GOAL: *To abstain from being sexually active as a teenager; to not use alcohol or other drugs*

Sex, alcohol, and drugs can be tempting. The pressure to be sexually active and get high can be almost irresistible at times. Especially if your friends are having sex, drinking, or using drugs, you may feel left out if you aren't, too.

You may think that you have to prove yourself by having sex. Or you might feel that the only way to keep a romantic partner interested in you is to have sex with him or her. Maybe you decide that you want someone in your life who really belongs to you—like a baby. And you're probably curious about alcohol and drugs.

Restraint requires courage—and support. Talk with your parents, teachers, youth leaders, religious leaders, and other adults you know and trust. Get the facts about STDs (sexually transmitted diseases), teen pregnancy, and what happens to kids who drink and use drugs. Think about and clarify your personal values, then surround yourself with friends who feel the way you do about sex, alcohol, and drugs.

Abstinence is a powerful way to show that you can control yourself and you respect yourself. Even if you've already had sex, or if you've been using alcohol or other drugs, you can stop. It's not too late. Young people who have chosen abstinence report that it's a big relief. You may want to try it and see for yourself.

SOCIAL COMPETENCIES

Young people need skills and competencies that equip them to make positive choices, build relationships, and succeed in life.

The five **social competencies assets** are:

32. Planning and Decision Making

33. Interpersonal Competence

34. Cultural Competence

35. Resistance Skills

36. Peaceful Conflict Resolution

The more personal skills a young person has, the more likely it is that he or she will grow up healthy.

ASSET #32
Planning and Decision Making

Kids know how to plan ahead and make choices.

33% of the kids we surveyed have this asset in their lives.

At Home

○ Have family meetings to talk about plans that affect the whole family. Invite suggestions from everyone, including the youngest children.

○ Give your teenager full responsibility for planning and preparing a family meal once a month.

○ Model planning and decision making. Have to-do lists and calendars visible in your home. Give your children daily planners or datebooks and demonstrate how to use them.

○ When your kids receive long-term assignments at school, offer to help them plan and make decisions in order to finish on time.

○ Give your teenager increasing responsibility for planning his or her own future. *Examples:* saving money for a special purchase; finding a summer job. Prompt good planning by asking questions, but don't take over the planning process.

⊙ Model choice making: (1) gathering information; (2) viewing the choice from all sides; (3) weighing potential consequences; (4) listing pros and cons; and (5) making a choice and sticking to it. Help your children apply this process to choices they're facing.

⊙ Talk your children through choices. Use "what if?" questions to help them anticipate consequences. *Example:* "What if you don't clean your room by Friday when your friend comes to spend the night?"

⊙ Allow for mistakes. Don't blow up at a poor choice, and don't rescue your child from the consequences, either.

⊙ Encourage your kids to keep a journal of the choices they make. Explain that they should write down what happened *and* how they felt at the time. This reinforces positive choices and serves as a strong reminder of the effects of negative choices.

⊙ Point out to your children that not making a choice *is* making a choice—it's choosing not to choose. Explain that this gives someone else the power to determine what happens next.

At School

⊙ Let students plan class projects, assignments, and even some schoolwide activities.

⊙ Teach planning and organizational skills. *Example:* When you assign a research paper, assign due dates for each step—choosing a topic, doing research, preparing an outline, writing a first draft, revising, and so on.

✪ Create assignment sheets for your students. Or, if your budget allows it, provide students with daily planners for the school year.

✪ Train staff to help students make long-term plans for continuing their education and choosing a career.

✪ Have students role-play making various types of decisions. Have them predict possible outcomes and consequences. Talk with them about decisions you've made and how they turned out.

✪ Ask students to talk about or write about tough choices they have made. Challenge them to articulate the reasons behind their choices.

✪ Include student leaders on decision-making committees and boards.

In the Community

✪ Have kids identify something in the community they'd like to change, then develop a plan for changing it. Take their plan seriously.

✪ Reserve room on a local cable channel for a calendar of youth activities and events, or post events on a community website.

✪ Offer workshops for community members on planning and decision-making skills.

✪ Permit young people to participate in decisions about community programs and special projects.

✪ Invite motivational speakers to talk to kids about important choices they have made.

○ Train adult leaders to help kids through the decision-making process.

In the Faith Community

○ Give young people an active role in planning the youth program. *Example:* If kids really want a basketball court on the parking lot, have them create a plan for making it happen.

○ Include young people in decisions that affect the faith community as a whole.

○ Invite kids to plan special events. Even young children can do this with adult guidance and supervision.

○ When appropriate, talk with young people about how their faith informs their decisions.

ASSET #33
Interpersonal Competence

Kids have empathy, sensitivity, and friendship skills.

48% of the kids we surveyed have this asset in their lives.

At Home

○ Practice interpersonal skills with your child, such as meeting people, starting conversations, asking questions, and finding similar interests. Be aware that when you and your child meet new people together, your child will be watching you to see how you handle the situation.

○ Practice seeing things from a child's perspective. Then you can truly empathize when your kids come to you with problems or concerns. You'll also be modeling empathy for them.

○ Go to a public place with your child. Together, try to guess what kinds of moods people are in by the way they walk and look.

○ When your children do things that hurt other people's feelings, talk with them about how their behavior affects others.

○ Invite people over for dinner often. Spend time as a family talking with your guests.

○ Welcome your children's friends into your home. Spend time talking with them and getting to know them.

○ Initiate conversations with your kids about relationships. Talk about your friendships; ask about theirs.

○ Emphasize the value of diversity in friendships. Encourage your kids to form friendships with people of different ages, ethnic origins, cultural backgrounds, economic circumstances, and faiths. Model this in your own friendships.

At School

○ Use role playing and creative visualization to teach empathy, sensitivity, and interpersonal skills.

○ Hold discussion groups about social and emotional experiences during lunch or after school. Encourage students to talk about their feelings and explore appropriate ways to express them.

○ Expose students to the life experiences of other people in concrete ways. *Example:* When discussing the 1970s in history class, invite a Vietnam veteran, a women's rights activist, or an environmental activist who lived through that time to talk with your class.

○ Use teaching styles that promote interaction and friendship-building.

○ Mix students in groups that reflect the diversity of your school. Kids who form friendships with a wide variety of people are less likely to develop prejudices.

✪ Encourage students to extend warm welcomes to new additions to your class or school. Remind them that everyone has been the "new kid" at one time or another, and ask them to remember how that feels.

✪ Talk with your students about the importance of friendship in your life. Share stories and anecdotes about your friends, things you've done together, and why your friends mean so much to you.

In the Community

✪ Greet kids and teens in the neighborhood and make time to talk with them. Get to know the family next door.

✪ Provide programs that bring children, teens, adults, and seniors together for fun and possible friendship.

✪ Emphasize cooperation over competition in activities and games.

✪ Take time to listen to kids express their feelings. Encourage them to listen to each other.

✪ Make youth programs inviting and accessible to a diversity (economic, ethnic, religious) of kids.

✪ Challenge kids and teens to reach out to newcomers and others who may not have friends or feel welcome in a group.

✪ Watch how young people interact with each other, and identify those who may need help with friendship skills. Train adult leaders to teach friendship skills.

✪ For activities, service projects, and special programs, mix young people in groups that reflect the diversity of your community.

In the Faith Community

○ As a faith community, model empathy and sensitivity toward each other, your community, and the world.

○ Sponsor service projects and mission trips that bring young people into contact with different cultures and traditions. Take time to reflect on the experiences so kids will internalize the feelings of empathy.

○ Start a discussion group on dating, making and keeping friends, and other relationship issues.

○ Plan social events to which young people may invite friends from outside the faith community.

○ Be a friendly faith community. Help new people and visitors feel welcome and accepted.

ASSET #34
Cultural Competence

Kids know and are comfortable with people of different cultural, racial, and/or ethnic backgrounds.

42% of the kids we surveyed have this asset in their lives.

At Home

✪ Teach your kids about their heritage. Encourage them to feel proud of their cultural, ethnic, and racial identity without feeling superior.

✪ Go as a family to events that celebrate different cultures and faith traditions. Talk about them afterward.

✪ Include traditions from many cultures in your family celebrations. Learn words from other languages; prepare meals from different cultures; listen to world music.

✪ Create a family environment that encourages positive discussion about differences. Don't tolerate jokes or other put-downs that demean people who are different.

✪ Expose your children to many kinds of people. Invite friends and neighbors from various cultures and backgrounds into your home.

✪ Examine images that television, movies, books, and websites project of people from various cultures. Discuss what's authentic and what's stereotypical and how you can determine the difference.

○ Encourage your child to get a pen pal from a different country.

○ Check yourself for subtle racist attitudes, biases, or prejudices. Work to overcome them. Talk with your children about racism, bias, and prejudice.

○ When your child has a negative reaction to a cultural or racial difference, don't ignore it. Immediately find out more about what happened and what your child is feeling. Ask questions to help your child figure out why he or she responded that way. Point out harmful, hurtful responses and suggest alternatives that promote cultural competence.

At School

○ Model acceptance and appreciation of differences. Make these stated values in your school and district. Don't tolerate racism, bias, or prejudice.

○ Educate teachers and other staff about respecting and working with cultural differences.

○ Include the accomplishments and thinking of diverse peoples in all subjects. Incorporate information (history, literature, art, music, biography, philosophy) from many cultures into the curriculum.

○ Provide activities that increase students' awareness and acceptance of differences.

○ Give students opportunities to share and celebrate their own heritage.

○ Teach students how to relate to people who are different from them.

In the Community

✪ Include the images and voices of a variety of people (men, women, young, old, black, white, Hispanic, Native American, Asian) in community publications, advertisements, posters, and promotional materials.

✪ Use local newspapers, magazines, TV, websites, and radio to educate residents about different cultures and customs within your community.

✪ Celebrate many types of cultural events within your community.

✪ Articulate clear community expectations that honor diversity. Don't tolerate racism, bias, or prejudice.

✪ Celebrate your community's diversity with a heritage festival.

✪ Support and expand programs that help deepen kids' understanding of and appreciation for their own roots. Encourage young people to embrace their heritage and claim their cultural strengths.

In the Faith Community

✪ Form a relationship with a faith community that's different from yours. Provide opportunities for members to meet, work together, serve together, and get to know each other.

✪ Make sure the materials used in your religious education classes reflect cultural diversity.

✪ Include information and traditions from many cultures in education classes and worship services.

✪ Invite members of other faith communities to join you for special celebrations and events. Or arrange for your youth groups to get together.

ASSET #35
Resistance Skills

Kids can resist negative peer pressure and avoid dangerous situations.

45% of the kids we surveyed have this asset in their lives.

At Home

○ Encourage your children to express their feelings, values, and beliefs at home. Allow them to disagree with you in a respectful way.

○ Talk with your child about different ways to resist. *Examples:* Walk away from the situation; calmly say no; say how you feel; use humor; stick up for yourself (be assertive); ignore the person or situation; confront the person; call a friend to help you; stay away from the situation from then on; invite a peer mediator to help; tell a caring adult. Which does your child like best? Least? Why?

○ Role-play with your child times when resistance skills are necessary. *Examples:* being pressured to have sex, drink alcohol, or use drugs; being asked to ride in a car with a person who has been drinking alcohol; being invited to a party at a friend's house when the parents are away; being called a coward because you won't shoplift; being called a traitor because you won't help a friend cheat on a test.

- Find out who your children's friends are. Get to know them.

- Talk with your children about peer pressure. Share stories from your own childhood and teen years.

- Teach your kids the differences between assertiveness, aggression, and passivity. Assertiveness is positive and affirming; aggression is negative and demanding; passivity makes one vulnerable. Role-play all three kinds of behavior with your children. Teach them assertiveness skills.

At School

- Encourage students to express their feelings, beliefs, values, and opinions without fear of being put down. Do not tolerate bullying behavior of any kind.

- Role-play difficult situations with students so they can practice and strengthen their resistance skills. Be open to opportunities to teach resistance skills. (See the second bullet under "At Home" on page 201.)

- Build resistance skills into health and prevention curricula. Talk with students about peer pressure.

- Train student leaders in ways to build resistance skills for themselves and their peers.

- Teach students the differences between assertiveness, aggression, and passivity. Model and role-play assertiveness skills. Encourage students to stick up for themselves.

- Show that you value assertiveness in your interactions with students—in the classroom, in teacher-student conferences, and on other occasions. Be willing to listen even when you disagree.

In the Community

✪ Provide opportunities for young people to express and act on their values and beliefs.

✪ Watch for opportunities in your encounters with kids to reinforce healthy behaviors and resistance skills.

✪ Send consistent messages encouraging young people to resist negative peer pressure and avoid dangerous situations. Ask the media to be partners in this effort. Ask kids what *they* think the messages should say. What language/approach is most likely to get through to kids instead of turning them off?

✪ Form teams of teens to teach resistance skills to younger kids. Use role play, drama, puppets, music, and art as tools in this process.

✪ Offer assertiveness training workshops and seminars for children, teens, and adults.

In the Faith Community

✪ Include resistance skills as part of your youth education programming.

✪ Help young people see their faith tradition as a resource in resisting negative peer pressure and avoiding dangerous situations.

✪ Role-play difficult situations with kids and teens so they can practice and strengthen their resistance skills. Be open to opportunities to teach resistance skills. (See the second bullet under "At Home" on page 201.)

✪ Start a discussion group for young people. Encourage them to talk about times when they have felt pressured to act in opposition to their beliefs.

ASSET #36
Peaceful Conflict Resolution

Kids seek to resolve conflicts nonviolently.

44% of the kids we surveyed have this asset in their lives.

At Home

✪ Model peaceful conflict resolution in your home.

✪ Learn and practice peaceful conflict resolution as a family. When a conflict arises: (1) Have everyone involved state their needs and wants without blaming others. (2) Have everyone really *listen* and try to understand each other. (3) Stay focused on the conflict at hand; don't bring up other conflicts. (4) Emphasize creative problem solving and new solutions. (5) Negotiate until you reach a win-win result.

✪ Allow family members to leave the discussion if they're too angry or upset to resolve the conflict peacefully. Agree on a time to reconvene and try again.

✪ Sit down together and talk about small conflicts before they become big problems.

○ Teach your kids how to use "I-messages." The basic formula for an "I-message" is "I feel _____ when _____ because _____. I want you to _____." *Example:* Instead of "You make me so mad when you borrow my jacket without asking," your child could say "*I feel* angry and upset *when* you borrow my jacket without asking, *because* then I can't wear it. *I want you to* ask me first."

○ Read books about peace and peaceful conflict resolution with your children. Ask your librarian for suggestions. Discuss what you read.

○ Set up a "Peace Place" in your home. This might be a room or a corner of a room where family members can go when they need to resolve a conflict. The rules of your Peace Place might be: (1) Go there if someone asks you to. (2) Use respectful words. (3) Take turns talking and listening. (4) Use "I-messages." (5) If the problem is too big for you to solve, get help.

○ Teach your children that hitting, pushing, kicking, and other violent behaviors are *not* okay. This goes for adults in the family, too.

At School

○ Include peacefulness in your school's stated values. Pass a petition calling for a peaceful school and invite everyone— students, teachers, administrators, staff—to sign it. Post it where all can see it every day.

○ Make conflict resolution training available to students, faculty, and support staff.

○ Institute and enforce strict anti-bullying rules.

✪ Set up a "Peace Place" in your classroom. You might broaden the description under "At Home" and make this a place where students can go anytime they want to be quiet, thoughtful, and calm. Have students decorate it with artwork and posters. Make books and soothing music available.

✪ Form a Peace Club at your school.

✪ Establish a peer mediation system so students can help each other resolve conflicts peacefully.

✪ Incorporate lessons about peace and peacemakers into the curriculum.

✪ Don't tolerate violence of any kind in your school.

In the Community

✪ Develop a shared community commitment to peaceful conflict resolution.

✪ Promote and publicize the efforts of community members who are working for peace.

✪ Support programs and organizations that work to reduce domestic violence and abuse.

✪ Offer mediation services to neighborhoods, families, and kids in need.

✪ Offer classes and workshops on conflict resolution. Make them available to parents, teens, children, and whole families.

In the Faith Community

- ✪ Teach conflict resolution skills to young people and adults. Include articles and suggestions in mailings to member households.

- ✪ Draw on your faith tradition's commitment to peace as you help young people build this asset.

- ✪ Have members share stories about times when they resolved conflicts peacefully.

- ✪ Establish a peer mediation system so kids and teens can help each other resolve conflicts peacefully.

ASSET BUILDING
IN ACTION

In Milton-Freewater, Oregon, apple orchards make up a crucial part of the local economy. Through a partnership between community schools and area businesses, colleges, and volunteers, high school students learned about the commitment, planning, and decision making it takes to manage an orchard—or any other local enterprise.

Each week, volunteers met with young people in greenhouses whose use had been donated by businesses. These volunteers demonstrated various aspects of agriculture, such as seed germination. Science teacher Diane Groff said participating students developed initiative, responsibility, and respect for living things, while also gaining field and research experience in a vital community industry. In addition, they built relationships with the volunteers. This not only expanded the students' skills, but also extended the network of important adults and role models in their lives.

Funds for this project came from environmentally related work that the students themselves took on. For example, students planted 3,000 young ivy plants to sell to the city. Then the teens planted the ivy as ground cover on local highway overpasses.

Tips for Teens

Build Your Own Assets

Asset #32: Planning and Decision Making

GOAL: *To know how to plan ahead and make choices*

Some kids take life one day at a time. That's great—until they miss an important deadline, opportunity, or party.

If you're a poor planner, start simple: Make a daily to-do list. Number the items, starting with 1 for most important. Check off items as you complete them. Move leftover items to the next day's list. Once you get the hang of this, buy a planning calendar. Inexpensive ones are available at every office supplies store. Or, check out online calendars and planning tools. Now you can start writing in future things to do—dates of long-term assignments, school holidays, upcoming social events, and whatever else you don't want to forget.

If you're already a great planner, put your skills to work and help plan something big: a school carnival, a community event, the first-ever talent show in your faith community. Keep a journal of your experience. Afterward, summarize it on a single page, with an emphasis on your own responsibilities and contributions. This will help you get a clearer sense of what you gained from the experience and what you might do the same way or differently the next time. It will also look very good to a prospective employer or college admissions officer.

Does it seem as if your parents make a lot of the decisions in your life, including some you'd like to make yourself? Ask if you can start making some decisions. If you prove that you're responsible, your parents will have more confidence in you. Are there some decisions that leave you feeling paralyzed? They may be too big for you to decide on your own. Get help from an adult you trust. This will give you more confidence about future decisions.

Asset #33: Interpersonal Competence

GOAL: *To know how to make and keep friends*

Friendships are built, in large part, on empathy and sensitivity: understanding that other people have needs and feelings, and being aware of and responsive to these needs and feelings. Empathy begins by deciding how you want to be treated—probably with kindness and respect. From there, it's not too hard to understand that other people want to be treated the same way. If you remember times when you were treated unkindly, or even cruelly, you can make a personal commitment not to say or do things that will cause pain to others. Similarly, think of times when someone has reached out to you or boosted your spirits, and remind yourself to make connections and be kind to others, too.

If you can't find friends in the usual places—school, your neighborhood, your place of worship—then look at your community as a whole. Is there a club or organization that matches one of your interests? Consider joining. You'll immediately have at least one thing in common with everyone else.

Start simply: Smile and say hi. Ask people about themselves, and tell them something about you. Invite people to do things with you—go to a movie, study in the library after school, help you with a volunteer project.

Make an effort to form friendships with many different kinds of people. Diversity makes life more interesting. Valuing and appreciating diversity—which happens naturally when your friends are different ages, ethnic backgrounds, genders, religions, and races—is an essential step toward eliminating bias and prejudice.

Asset #34: Cultural Competence

GOAL: *To know and feel comfortable around people of different cultural, racial, and/or ethnic backgrounds*

If you already have this asset, you're probably enjoying the benefits. You get along with all kinds of people; you don't suspect or fear differences; you're not limited by ignorance or prejudice; and you're open to many different types of experiences.

If you don't have this asset, you're going to need it, because the world is growing more diverse each day. Here are some ways you can start building this asset for yourself:

▸ Be willing to meet new people, and make a special effort to meet people who are different from you.

▸ Watch TV shows and movies that positively portray people from different cultural, racial, and/or ethnic backgrounds.

▸ Listen to music from a variety of other cultures.

▸ Listen when other people talk positively about friends and neighbors from other cultures.

▸ Read positive books and stories about people from many different cultures.

▸ Eat at ethnic restaurants or prepare ethnic meals for your family.

▸ Attend cross-cultural events with your family, your friends, or on your own.

▸ Choose classes and projects at school that expose you to a variety of cultures, traditions, heritages, and belief systems.

As you're learning about differences, look for similarities—the common ground on which relationships are built. Practically overnight, your life will be more interesting, and you'll be better prepared to succeed in our changing world.

Asset #35: Resistance Skills

GOAL: *To resist negative peer pressure and avoid dangerous situations*

Before you can decide what you *won't* do, you need to be clear on what you believe—and why. Talk with an adult you trust about your values and beliefs. Or make a list on your own. Start each list item with "I believe. . . ." Then read through your whole list, make any changes, and keep revising until it feels right to you. Now you know what to stick up for, say no to, and say yes to.

Resisting negative peer pressure and avoiding dangerous situations takes assertiveness skills. When you're assertive, you're firm yet respectful. You don't bully or back down. You state your position calmly and don't budge from it even when you're teased, mocked, or threatened. *Examples:* "No, I don't do drugs." "No, I don't drink." "No, I don't go to parties when parents aren't around." "No, I don't ride with drivers who have been drinking. I'll find another way home."

Don't wait until you're in a tough situation to assert yourself. Do it earlier, when the stakes aren't as high. For example, when you're trying to choose a movie with your friends, speak up about the one you really want to see. Try not to start a confrontation; just calmly and honestly share your views and feelings.

Think of three people you can count on to be there for you and support your values and beliefs. Ask them to be your safety net—people you can call when you're pressured or tempted to do something unsafe or unhealthy. Keep their telephone numbers with you at all times. Offer to be a friend's safety net.

Asset #36: Peaceful Conflict Resolution

GOAL: *To resolve conflicts nonviolently whenever possible*

If your school or community offers conflict resolution training, get involved. If there's a peer mediation program at your school, sign up. Learn everything you can about resolving conflicts peacefully. Teach what you learn to younger kids.

You can build your own conflict resolution skills. Start by thinking about a time in your past when you were involved in a major conflict. What was it about? What was your view of the situation? What was the other person's view? Were you able to resolve the conflict peacefully? Why or why not? If you got involved in a similar conflict today, would you do anything differently? Did you learn anything that might help you *prevent* future conflicts?

With your family and friends, role-play different ways to resolve conflicts. Form the habit of saying what you want, need, and feel without blaming other people. Try talking about problems *before* they grow into conflicts. Practice using "I-messages." Instead of saying "YOU make me so mad" or "it's YOUR fault" or "YOU shouldn't have done that" or "YOU always . . . ," try saying "I feel _____ when _____ because _____. I want you to _____." (*Example:* "*I feel* angry *when* we make plans to go to a movie together and you're late, *because* then we miss the beginning. *I want you to* try to be on time, okay?") Be a good listener. Look at other people when they're speaking; acknowledge what they're saying; don't interrupt, but ask questions if you need more information. Many conflicts fade away when people really *listen* to each other.

POSITIVE IDENTITY

Young people need a strong sense of their own power, purpose, worth, and promise.

The four **positive identity assets** are:

37. Personal Power

38. Self-Esteem

39. Sense of Purpose

40. Positive View of Personal Future

The more a child has a sense of power, purpose, worth, and promise, the more likely it is that she or he will grow up healthy.

ASSET #37
Personal Power

Kids feel that they have control over many things that happen to them.

45% of the kids we surveyed have this asset in their lives.

At Home

○ Express confidence in your children's abilities. Children who trust their own abilities have personal power.

○ Help your children understand the difference(s) between what we can and can't control. *Example:* We can control what we say and do; we can't control what other people say and do.

○ Encourage kids to find solutions when problems arise. Keep asking "What can you do about this?"

○ Involve children of all ages in family decision making.

○ Give kids age-appropriate choices at all stages of their lives.

○ Encourage family members to point out "victim mentality comments" and "personal power comments" when family members tell about their day. *Examples:* "Sarah made me talk in class and I got into trouble" is a victim mentality comment. "Other kids teased Jacob but I didn't go along" is a personal power comment.

- Help family members form healthy lifestyle habits. Taking good care of oneself is an excellent way to develop personal power.

- Work to build social competencies in your child (see assets #32–36). Kids who are socially competent are more likely to feel a sense of personal power.

- Encourage your children to serve others (see assets #26 and #27). Kids who believe they can make a difference in the world have an enormous sense of personal power.

At School

- Talk with students about times when they felt powerless and times when they felt powerful. What made the difference? When they felt powerless, was it because they had no choices? When they felt powerful, was it because they had choices?

- Whenever it's realistic to do so, give students choices—about which assignment to do, which project to work on, whether to write an essay or a poem.

- Reinforce the message of "the power of one" to make a difference, using real-life stories of people who have overcome adversity, spoken out, or changed the lives of others.

- Emphasize each student's ability to control his or her own behavior. Get help for students who have difficulty doing this.

- Provide a suggestion box for your classroom or school. Invite students to make suggestions for improving the school. Implement as many suggestions as possible, and recognize the students who contributed the ideas.

- Actively involve students in decision making within the school. Whenever appropriate, invite their participation in determining issues of school climate, school policies, special activities, and curriculum.

✪ Help teachers find ways to maintain order in the classroom without overcontrolling their students.

In the Community

✪ Recognize and affirm young people who demonstrate good judgment.

✪ Model personal power by voting, speaking out about issues that matter to you, and being a problem solver.

✪ Include problem-solving skills in job training for teen workers.

✪ Involve kids in addressing youth issues and policies in the community. Give them useful roles and show that you value their contributions.

✪ Train adults who work with young people to affirm their abilities and give them choices whenever possible.

In the Faith Community

✪ Make children and teens a vital, contributing part of your faith community by involving them in planning and decision making.

✪ Give kids a say in planning activities for the youth program.

✪ Provide young people with many options for involvement so they can choose whatever best fits them and their interests or needs.

✪ Provide children and teens with opportunities to serve others. Let them know they have the power to make a difference.

ASSET #38
Self-Esteem

Kids feel good about themselves.

52% of the kids we surveyed have this asset in their lives.

At Home

○ Express your love for your children regularly and often. Show them and tell them every day how much they mean to you.

○ Write specific things you like about your child on sticky notes. Hide them around your child's room.

○ Celebrate each child's uniqueness. Find something special to value and affirm, whether it's a sense of humor, computer skills, singing voice, or wonderful smile.

○ When your kids make mistakes or bad choices, separate the deed from the doer. The *choice* is bad, not the child.

○ Treat your children with respect. Listen without interrupting; talk without yelling.

○ When your kids ask for something and you say no, treat them with respect and courtesy. Do your best to give an honest and reasonable explanation for your decision.

✪ Encourage your children to keep a journal of their accomplishments. This eventually becomes a "savings account" of positive feelings. Or keep a family "We did it!" journal. At family meetings, have family members individually name things they've accomplished, or things they've noticed other family members accomplish. Periodically celebrate these successes.

At School

✪ Use grading as an opportunity to affirm. This doesn't mean giving students grades they don't deserve. Instead, grade honestly, then add positive comments.

✪ Critique papers, reports, and tests constructively. Offer suggestions for improvements. Add positive comments.

✪ Take students seriously. Ask for their opinions; listen to their comments and suggestions; affirm their abilities and achievements.

✪ Teach students to accept criticism and respond to it in constructive ways.

✪ Treat all students with respect. Encourage everyone to contribute to class discussions. Identify and affirm individual talents.

In the Community

✪ Take time to pay attention to young people—for example, while waiting in line at the grocery store or the movie theater. Demonstrate by your attitude and behavior that you value them and enjoy talking with them.

- Offer classes and workshops for young people on developing and strengthening self-esteem. Topics might include positive self-talk, learning from mistakes, accepting compliments, and asking for what they need.

- Invite experts to speak to parents about building self-esteem in kids.

- Involve young people in planning community events. Celebrate their accomplishment afterward.

In the Faith Community

- Accept and affirm all young people for who they are. Recognize and affirm individual talents, abilities, and accomplishments.

- Hold workshops and seminars for parents on building self-esteem in their children.

- Feature brief biographies in the worship bulletin of young people in your faith community.

- Learn the names of young people in your faith community and greet them as individuals when you see them.

ASSET #39
Sense of Purpose

Kids believe that their life has a purpose.

63% of the kids we surveyed have this asset in their lives.

At Home

✪ Model what it means to have a sense of purpose in life. Do things that matter to you; develop your talents; pursue your dreams. Share your sense of purpose with your children. Make it clear that you believe your life has meaning.

✪ Post inspiring quotations on the refrigerator and point them out to your children. Explain how those particular quotations affirm your values, motivate you, and help you remain purposeful. Invite your kids to find and post quotations of their own.

✪ Limit TV, computer, Internet, and telephone time. Encourage your children to use that time to develop and pursue their own interests.

✪ Have each family member list five things he or she is passionate about. Compare and discuss your family's "passion lists." Are there any surprises? If two family members share a passion, can they explore it together?

✪ Listen to your kids when they talk about their dreams. Get excited with them. Ask how you can help them pursue these dreams and interests.

✪ Encourage your children to get involved in activities that build on their talents and interests. Network with other adults and also young people who have similar talents and interests. See if you can participate in meaningful activities together.

✪ Together with your child, interview a neighbor or family member who seems to have a strong sense of purpose. How did he or she find that purpose? What does it take for him or her to maintain it?

✪ Give your children opportunities to find meaning in ways that are consistent with your family's values. This might involve service, religious activities, political involvement, or other pursuits.

At School

✪ Encourage students to write down their dreams and goals, both short-term and long-term. Check in with them periodically to see how it's going. Let them know it's okay to revise their goals and set new ones.

✪ Help students see a purpose in everything they're learning in school. *Example:* Why read literature? Because it deepens our understanding of other people and ourselves.

✪ Draw connections between classroom learning and significant opportunities, needs, and issues in the world.

✪ Have students read books and stories that tell about difficulties overcome and dreams achieved.

✪ Give students opportunities to reflect on and shape their own future.

❂ Include service learning as part of the regular school curriculum. Students who make a difference in the world *know* that their lives have meaning and purpose.

In the Community

❂ Involve kids and teens in volunteer activities. Recognize their skills, talents, and contributions.

❂ Invite young people you know to tell you about their dreams. Offer encouragement and advice. Be a mentor for kids and teens whose dreams are related to your own life's purpose and areas of expertise.

❂ Provide meaningful opportunities for young people to contribute to community life.

❂ Highlight community members who have contributed to community life in significant ways.

In the Faith Community

❂ Speak explicitly to kids about creating meaning in their lives and how that translates into daily activities, career choices, relationships, and behaviors.

❂ Encourage young people to reflect on, question, and develop their own values.

❂ Use religious education classes, sermons, and homilies to emphasize the importance of finding meaning and purpose in life.

❂ Help kids and teens identify, nurture, and celebrate their gifts. Provide opportunities for them to build on their interests and talents.

ASSET #40
Positive View of Personal Future

Kids are optimistic about their own future.

75% of the kids we surveyed have this asset in their lives.

At Home

○ Inspire hope by being hopeful, optimism by being optimistic. Look forward to your future and the future of your family with joyful anticipation.

○ Don't dismiss your children's dreams as naive or unrealistic. Instead, encourage them to tell you their dreams. Share in their enthusiasm. Help them make plans to realize their dreams.

○ Eliminate pessimistic phrases from your family vocabulary. Replace "It won't work" with "Why not try it?" Instead of "You can't do that by yourself," try "I can help you do that."

○ Pay particular attention to signs of hope in your community and the world. Don't just focus on all of the things that are wrong about the present or frightening about the future.

○ Together with your children, draw pictures of your fears about the future. Talk about them . . . and then rip them up. Discuss how you have the power to deal with difficult, scary, and painful situations when they arise.

○ Take time to enjoy life. Notice and appreciate a beautiful sunset, a good dinner, a funny show on television, a cute pet, a flower in your garden, a song heard on the radio. Share your joy with your children.

○ Be spontaneous. Drop everything to play ball, take a walk, catch a movie, or play a game with your kids. Spontaneity is essentially hopeful; you choose to do something suddenly because you expect to have a good time.

At School

○ Encourage and support students in pursuing their dreams.

○ Expose students to positive role models whose backgrounds are similar to theirs. This is especially important for students who come from troubled or economically disadvantaged families. It gives them hope for their own future.

○ Create a climate of optimism. Expect your students to succeed. Even a low grade can be accompanied by an encouraging note: "I know you'll do better next time."

○ Invite students to talk about their dreams and goals for the future.

In the Community

○ Help young people set personal goals that inspire hope.

○ Encourage kids to name their fears—things that might stop them from reaching their goals. Once fears are named, they can be addressed and dealt with.

○ Affirm and publicize the good things about your community. Be optimistic about its future.

○ Make a public statement about your community's commitment to the well-being of young people. Make a list of ways your community will work toward this commitment. Have it printed in your local newspaper, or post it on your community's website. This will help inspire community-wide optimism.

In the Faith Community

○ Encourage kids to talk about their hopes and dreams.

○ Pass on to young people the hope that is integral to your faith tradition.

○ Do projects that point to a more hopeful future. Instead of always addressing problems, identify areas of hope and creativity and encourage kids to get involved.

ASSET BUILDING
IN ACTION

"Imani Circle." "Kuumba Class." "Lion's Den." These phrases represent the philosophy of the Brother to Brother Program at Liberty Hill Baptist Church in Little Rock, Arkansas. This program—serving a neighborhood facing poverty and high crime rates—arose from the idea that helping young African-American males connect to their cultural roots is critical to their health and happiness.

Brother to Brother was carefully designed to provide young men with structure, support, and opportunities, all within a setting of positive identity and cultural heritage. Imani Circle (named after the Swahili word for faith) was a sharing and affirmation time. In Kuumba Class (Kuumba is the Swahili word for creativity), the boys made masks, molded figures, and did other arts and crafts. The Lion's Den was a recreation room.

"As black males, [these young men] feel stigmatized in the school and community," said program director Jimmy Cunningham. "In a world that is increasingly multicultural . . . it becomes even more important to be comfortable and grounded in self so you can relate to other people." The asset-building Brother to Brother program, Cunningham says, has helped these kids "become much more grounded and much more rooted."

Tips for Teens

Build Your Own Assets

Asset #37: Personal Power

GOAL: *To feel that you have control over many things that happen to you*

When you have personal power, you feel secure about who you are, and confident in yourself. You know that you have choices; you know that you can make decisions; you have a clear understanding of what you can and can't control.

When you have personal power, if something good happens to you, you don't think "I guess I'm just lucky." You know that you contributed to making it happen. Good grades don't fall out of the sky; good friendships don't form on their own. You *earn* the grades and *build* the friendships.

On the flip side, if something bad happens to you, you don't think "It's my fault; I deserve this; I'm a terrible person." Instead, you focus on positive steps you can take to remedy the situation.

If you believe that too many things in your life are controlled by others, you can do something about it. Talk to your parents, your teachers, and other adults who have power over you. See if they will agree to let you make more choices. Then, when you make a choice, follow through. Do what you say you will do. This shows that you're responsible and mature—someone other people can count on. And this usually leads to even *more* opportunities to make choices for yourself.

Asset #38: Self-Esteem

GOAL: *To feel good about yourself*

Self-talk—the messages we give ourselves—can have a big effect on our self-esteem. When you make a mistake, what do you tell yourself? "It's no big deal; everybody makes mistakes"? Or "How could I be so stupid? I can't believe I did that." When you succeed at something, do you say to yourself "Yes! I did it!" Or do you say "I could have done better." In each example, the first statement is a self-esteem booster; the second is a self-esteem smasher.

Whenever you have a negative thought about yourself—when your self-talk makes you feel bad—try changing it to a positive thought. Do this immediately. You'll feel better. Plus, you'll be forming the habit of self-affirmation, which most successful people share.

Asset #39: Sense of Purpose

GOAL: *To believe that your life has a purpose*

Do you believe that your life has a purpose? If you do, then you already have this important asset. Keep strengthening it through the choices you make and the actions you take. Stay focused on your purpose and don't let anyone or anything distract you from it. On the other hand, know that people and purposes can change. Don't lock yourself into following a goal or a dream that no longer seems right to you.

If you don't feel as though your life has a purpose, or you can't figure out what your purpose might be, find some quiet time and just think. Ask yourself what really matters to you. What gets you excited about each new day? What dreams do you have for the future? What are your talents? Interests? Passions? Where would you like to be—what would you like to be doing—five years from now? Ten years from now? If you could do only *one* thing with your life, what would it be?

Questions like these can help you find a purpose, because *you do have a purpose.* Every life has meaning. If you're still not convinced—if you really, truly can't imagine why you're here—then talk with an adult you trust and respect. Try to find someone who seems to have a strong purpose in life. Explain how you feel, and ask this person for help or support in finding your own purpose.

Asset #40: Positive View of Personal Future

GOAL: *To feel optimistic about your personal future*

What do you see when you envision your future? Are you happy or sad? In a job you enjoy or bored out of your mind? Do you have healthy, loving relationships, or are you lonely?

Studies have shown that when people picture themselves reaching their goals, they improve their chances of this really happening. Their dreams are more likely to come true. That's one reason why it's important for you to picture a positive future for yourself. Even if you don't know exactly *how* you'll achieve the things you dream of and long for, try to see them in your mind. Let your hope inspire you and guide you.

And remember: one way to create a positive future for yourself is to keep building your own Developmental Assets. If you've been reading the "Tips for Teens" sections throughout this book, then you know which assets you already have and which ones you need to work on. The more assets you have, the better.

Overcoming the Challenges to Asset Building

For some kids, building Developmental Assets is relatively easy. When children and teens have strong families and communities—when they're surrounded by caring, loving people—not much stands in the way of their building assets and benefiting from the positive opportunities they encounter in life. But what about kids who don't fit this description? Some have been victimized by abuse. Others are growing up in poverty and may not have access to many positive activities and influences. Some are so bombarded with harmful influences—bullying, stress, isolation, negative peer pressure, negative values—that the positive influences can't get through.

In our nationwide surveys, we have also identified and measured a number of roadblocks to success for young people. We call these **developmental deficits.** The more deficits a child has, the less likely it is that he or she will build large numbers of assets. As a result, the child will be much more likely to make negative decisions and choices, and to engage in risky behaviors.

The five main deficits we've surveyed over the years are:

1. Spending two or more hours each school day alone at home without an adult

2. Watching more than three hours of television or videos a day

3. Going to parties where friends/peers will be drinking alcohol or using drugs

4. Being physically abused by someone in the family or home

5. Being a victim of violence outside the home

A lack of economic security can also undermine efforts to build assets. How can young people benefit from music or drawing lessons if they can't afford them? What good does it do to want to go to college if you can't pay for field trips in school? How can you be alert in school if you don't get enough to eat? How can parents build a strong, caring family if they have to work two jobs just to make ends meet?

These are serious, difficult questions that we must address as a society if we really want kids to succeed. So, while we concentrate on building assets, we must also make determined efforts to prevent deficits—to break down these roadblocks to health and well-being.

Helping Kids Overcome Deficits

Amid the bad news of deficits, there's also good news: Some young people beat the odds. Having deficits doesn't necessarily doom kids to failure. In spite of the barriers, some young people thrive. Why? Because they have important assets in their lives that balance out and even overcome the deficits.

There are five things that seem to make the most difference for young people with deficits:

1. Getting them involved in structured, adult-led activities

2. Setting boundaries and limits

3. Nurturing a strong commitment to education

4. Providing support and care in all areas of their lives, not just in the family

5. Cultivating positive values and concern for others

While it may not be as easy for these kids to build assets, they can do it. This doesn't always involve taking them out of a difficult situation, as much as we'd sometimes like to be able to do that. It doesn't always involve a lot of money. What seems to matter most is the presence of caring people who are cheering for them, giving them opportunities, and believing in them. Kids who have this kind of support can bounce back in amazing ways and live amazing lives.

Forming an Asset Mindset

We know that assets can change kids' lives. Our research has shown again and again that when young people have enough of the Developmental Assets, both internal and external, they're much *more* likely to lead healthy, positive, productive lives. And they're much *less* likely to get involved in risky behaviors. Building assets in young people will more than pay off in the long run. It will help us, as a society, to spend less of our time and resources on crises and problems. But first, as a society, we must build an asset mindset.

You've probably heard this traditional African proverb: "It takes a whole village to raise a child." In other words, it's not enough for young people to hear a positive message at home *or* at school *or* in the community *or* at their place of worship. They need to hear the same message reinforced in all areas of their lives. *What Kids Need to Succeed* includes ideas for parents *and* schools *and* communities *and* faith communities— and teens themselves, because young people can build their own assets. Everyone has the potential to be an asset builder.

Asset Building on Your Own: Eight Ideas

1. **Read (or reread) "What Do Kids Really Need?" on pages 1–20 of this book.** Look at the charts that illustrate the power of the assets to reduce risky behaviors and increase positive behaviors. Start telling other people about the importance of building assets for kids and teens.

2. **Start reading stories about young people from a new perspective.** When you read success stories about kids in the media or online, try to identify which assets are present in their lives. When you read stories about kids with problems, think about which assets might be missing for them. How can you build those assets in your community?

3. **Meet with a colleague, teacher, school counselor, social worker, religious leader, or youth worker you know.** Ask him or her to talk about his or her needs, interests, and concerns for your community. Introduce the concept of building assets in young people. Get his or her perspective. Bounce ideas around.

4. **Think about how you approach young people.** When you work with kids and teens in your own family, school, community group, or faith community, do you focus most of your energy on intervening in crises, preventing problems, or promoting assets? How can you shift more of your energy to asset building?

5. **Share your thinking at a community meeting or event.** Give people a chance to react and talk about the potential of what you have just described. Brainstorm ways your community can work together to build assets.

6. **Affirm asset-building gestures and efforts you see others make.** Tell people that their actions are positive and powerful—that they are helping kids succeed.

7. **Look at the list of 40 assets at least once a week and commit to at least one act of asset building every day.** Or . . .

8. Commit to building one asset. Choose one that's important to you and make it a priority in your life. *Examples:* You might become a mentor for a young person in your community. Or you might commit to spending more time at home with your children. Or you might undertake a family service project. Or you may decide just to be nicer to the kids in your neighborhood—to see and hear them, acknowledge and interact with them rather than ignoring them.

No one person alone can change a whole community, but everyone individually can make a significant difference.

Communities Working Together

In our experience with asset building in many different communities, we've learned some important lessons about building assets. We know that your personal commitment is key. But it's also important that people begin thinking about how everyone *together* can build assets. How do we create neighborhoods, towns, cities, states, and even nations that make it a top priority to build assets in children and teens? There's probably no single strategy that would work everywhere. But as communities have started asking that question, they've discovered some powerful principles that are shaping what they do.

Everyone has a role to play. Not just parents, schools, community organizations, faith communities, or governments, though they all certainly play important roles. *Everyone* can get involved in asset building. Senior citizens and children, single adults and couples, policy makers and citizens, neighbors and employers, wealthy families and low-income families, liberals and conservatives—kids need us all. And we all can share a common, hopeful commitment to kids and the future.

Asset building is more about people than programs. Relationships are the key. Quality relationships can form with or without a program—a neighbor playing basketball with the kids, a grandmother keeping an eye on the bus stop to make sure children get off to school safely. Programs may be vehicles for connecting young people to adults, but the critical issue is the care and support that grow through relationships. Money may help sometimes, but the commitment and involvement of caring people make the biggest difference.

Asset building unleashes untapped resources. Most people really do care about kids; they just don't know how to express that care in tangible ways. Most communities have great services for children and families, but they're all going in so many directions that they can compete and conflict with each other. Asset building gives people and organizations a clear, positive focus for their energy and resources.

All kids need asset building. Often youth programming focuses on just the "best" kids or the "worst" kids—the high achievers or the young people at risk. True, these groups may need special attention in some areas. But asset building can help all kids. Communities are discovering the importance of designing strategies that can benefit a broad cross-section of kids, not just a targeted few.

Every community can improve. Search Institute has studied hundreds of communities. While each community is different, all communities—regardless of region or size— would be better off with higher levels of assets. Instead of trying to figure out who has more problems where, we all need to learn from each other.

Asset Building in Your Community: Eight Principles

1. **Engage people from throughout the community.** Because the asset-building vision calls for community-wide responsibility for youth, it's important to involve many different stakeholders from the outset. A mixture of motivated citizens and their leaders provides a good balance. Many communities have developed "vision teams" with representatives from all sectors—schools, government, law enforcement, faith communities, service agencies, businesses, healthcare providers, and so on—along with young people, parents, and other citizens, including seniors and people from various racial/ethnic and socioeconomic groups.

2. **Start with a clear and positive vision.** The typical community-wide effort is initiated because of a crisis. Too often, however, these initiatives deal with the immediate crisis but lack the energy or vision to sustain them. A positive vision can energize a community for the long term. It can also help groups set aside political and ideological agendas and focus, instead, on their shared commitment to the well-being of children and adolescents.

3. **Build on reliable information.** Many communities find that a survey of young people can be a catalyst for creative and sustained action. Clear, reliable information gives people a shared reference point for reflecting on the needs, realities, and resources in the community as they shape their vision for the future. Otherwise, you risk shaping a vision and agenda that don't adequately capture the needs, issues, and possibilities in the community for children and adolescents.

4. **Resist the temptation to create new programs.** Because most responses to youth issues in recent decades have been programmatic, intentional energy will be needed to avoid simply developing another program to respond to a specific need. The most important tasks for the "vision bearers" for asset building are to keep the vision of a healthy community alive and to prompt individuals and institutions to discover ways they can integrate asset building into their own missions and commitments.

5. **Take time to motivate and educate.** Because asset building is a fairly new and nontraditional way of thinking about communities and young people, it's important not to assume that everyone automatically understands the framework and its implications. Unless people internalize the many dimensions of the asset framework, asset building risks becoming a shallow campaign to "be nice to kids." Repeating key messages about assets lays a foundation for a more thoughtful, well-rounded response.

6. **Celebrate commitments and successes.** Asset building is a long-term vision, not a quick fix. But as communities embark on this journey, it's important to notice, celebrate, and talk about the landmarks along the way: the new awareness of young people, the shifts in conversations, the shared enthusiasm and commitments. These stories renew energy and refocus commitment.

7. **Embrace innovations from the community.** Once people are aligned with the vision of asset building, their creativity in finding ways to nurture assets can be startling. Encouraging this innovation is key to breaking out of old patterns and discovering fresh approaches to rebuilding community for kids.

   One example of grassroots innovation is in place in Maine. Instead of being punished through the court system, first-time, nonviolent youth offenders must take a class in which they learn about what kids need to grow up healthy. In the program, called "Jump Start," each young person is paired with a volunteer mentor who lends support throughout the eight-week period. Young people who have taken the course have formed an alumni group to reinforce the positive messages they learned.

8. **Network with other communities.** While many communities have begun asset-building initiatives, no one knows all the answers yet. No one knows exactly how everything will work. But each community is learning something new each day. Network with others. Share stories and ideas. Explore challenges. Together, we'll continue learning what works—and what doesn't work—to bring the vision closer to reality.

Asset-Strong Communities

As more and more communities everywhere start building assets, each community will remain unique in some ways, reflecting the personalities and priorities of the people who live there. But there are some things that likely will be in place in all asset-strong communities:

▸ Parents will have access to parent education and support that strengthens families and gives them skills in asset building.

▸ Youth programs will make special efforts to ensure that all young people are involved in positive, constructive activities.

▸ Communities will develop a consensus on what's important to them—the positive values and norms they hope to pass on to the next generation.

▸ Teens will be seen as leaders and contributors in the community.

▸ Age segregation will be minimized so that kids regularly interact with people of all ages.

▸ Youth employers, teachers, and coaches will all have training in asset building.

▸ Schools will pay as much attention to the school climate as they do to the academic curriculum.

▸ Various organizations in the community that usually operate separately from each other—government, business, schools, families, faith communities—will all cooperate on behalf of kids.

These are only a few of the benefits of asset building. Dozens of other good things are likely to occur as more communities become asset-strong. The commitment to helping kids succeed is powerful—and it's contagious. And the more people in your community and others catch the vision and join the asset-building team, the brighter the future will be—not just for kids, but for all of us.

Resources for Asset Building

Almost any good book or website on parenting, teaching, or guiding kids contains information you can use to build assets in young people. As you become more involved in asset building, you'll probably want to visit your local library or bookstore for additional resources. What follows are selective lists of titles and sites that we recommend.

Resources for Parents

Books

Benson, Peter L., *Sparks: How Parents Can Help Ignite the Hidden Strengths of Teenagers* (San Francisco: Jossey-Bass, 2008).

Brooks, Robert, and Sam Goldstein, *Raising a Self-Disciplined Child: Help Your Child Become More Responsible, Confident, and Resilient* (New York: McGraw-Hill, 2007).

Charter, Christine, *Raising Happiness: 10 Simple Steps for More Joyful Kids and Happier Parents* (New York: Ballantine Books, 2010).

David, Laurie, and Kristin Uhrenholdt, *The Family Dinner: Great Ways to Connect with Your Kids, One Meal at a Time* (New York: Grand Central Life & Style, 2003).

Dinkmeyer, Don, Sr., Gary D. McKay, and Don Dinkmeyer, Jr., *The Parent's Handbook: Systematic Training for Effective Parenting* (Bowling Green, KY: STEP Publishers, 2007).

Edelman, Marian Wright, *The Measure of Our Success: A Letter to My Children and Yours* (New York: HarperCollins, 1993).

Elium, Don, and Jeanne Elium, *Raising a Son: Parents and the Making of a Healthy Man*, Third Edition (Berkeley, CA: Celestial Arts, 2004).

Elium, Jeanne, and Don Elium, *Raising a Daughter: Parents and the Awakening of a Healthy Woman,* Revised Edition (Berkeley, CA: Celestial Arts, 2003).

Feinstein, Sheryl, *Inside the Teenage Brain: Parenting a Work in Progress* (Lanham, MD: Rowman & Littlefield Education, 2009).

Gottman, John, *The Heart of Parenting: How to Raise an Emotionally Intelligent Child* (New York: Fireside, 1998).

Kindlon, Dan, and Michael Thompson, *Raising Cain: Protecting the Emotional Life of Boys* (New York: Ballantine Books, 2000).

Metcalf, Linda, *Parenting Toward Solutions: How Parents Can Use the Skills They Already Have to Raise Responsible, Loving Kids* (Englewood Cliffs, NJ: Prentice Hall, 1997).

Nelsen, Jane, and Lynn Lott, *Positive Discipline for Teenagers: Empowering Your Teen and Yourself Through Kind and Firm Parenting* (New York: Three Rivers Press, 2000).

Payne, Kim John, and Lisa M. Ross, *Simplicity Parenting: Using the Extraordinary Power of Less to Raise Calmer, Happier, and More Secure Kids* (New York: Ballantine Books, 2009).

Pipher, Mary, *Reviving Ophelia: Saving the Selves of Adolescent Girls* (New York: Riverhead Trade, 2005).

Riera, Michael, *Staying Connected to Your Teenager: How to Keep Them Talking to You and How to Hear What They're Really Saying* (Cambridge, MA: Da Capo Press, 2003).

Steinberg, Laurence, and Ann Levine, *You and Your Adolescent: The Essential Guide for Ages 10–25*, New and Revised Edition (New York: Simon & Schuster, 2011).

Walsh, David, *No: Why Kids—of All Ages—Need to Hear It and Ways Parents Can Say It* (New York: Free Press, 2007).

———*Smart Parenting, Smarter Kids* (New York: Free Press, 2011).

———*Why Do They Act That Way? A Survival Guide to the Adolescent Brain for You and Your Teen* (New York: Free Press, 2004).

Weinstein, Miriam, *The Surprising Power of Family Meals: How Eating Together Makes Us Smarter, Stronger, Healthier, and Happier* (Hanover, NH: Steerforth Press, 2006).

Wolf, Anthony E., *Get Out of My Life, But First Could You Drive Me and Cheryl to the Mall? A Parent's Guide to the New Teenager* (New York: Farrar, Straus & Giroux, 2002).

Websites

Conversation Generation: Teens and Parents Talking (www.hhs.gov/ash/ oah/resources-and-publications/info/parents/) This website from the U.S. Office of Adolescent Health (OAH) provides extensive information on a variety of tough topics, with an emphasis on helping parents and teens talk honestly about sexuality and related issues. The OAH website also includes information on Developmental Assets.

NYU Child Studies Center (www.aboutourkids.org/families) This site offers extensive parenting information, including on medical and developmental topics.

ParentFurther (www.ParentFurther.com) From Search Institute, this website helps parents take everyday steps to address the challenges of parenting with an asset-building approach. A free email newsletter with parenting tips is also available through the site.

Resources for Schools

Books

Comer, James, *Waiting for a Miracle: Why Schools Can't Solve Our Problems—and How We Can* (New York: Dutton, 1997).

Curwin, Dr. Richard, *Rediscovering Hope: Our Greatest Teaching Strategy* (Bloomington, IN: National Educational Service, 1992).

Drew, Naomi, *Learning the Skills of Peacemaking: An Activity Guide for Elementary-Age Children on Communicating, Cooperating, Resolving Conflict,* Revised and Expanded (Torrance, CA: Jalmar Press, 1995).

Mendler, Dr. Allen, *What Do I Do When . . . ? How to Achieve Discipline with Dignity in the Classroom* (Bloomington, IN: Solution Tree, 2007).

Nelsen, Jane, and H. Stephen Glenn, *Time Out: A Guide for Parents and Teachers Using Popular Discipline Methods to Empower and Encourage Children* (Fair Oaks, CA: Sunrise Press, 1992).

Sizer, Theodore R., and Nancy Faust Sizer, *The Students Are Watching: Schools and the Moral Contract* (Boston: Beacon Press, 1999).

Whitaker, Todd, *What Great Teachers Do Differently: 14 Things That Matter Most* (Larchmont, NY: Eye On Education, 2004).

Websites

CASEL: Collaborative for Academic, Social, and Emotional Learning (www.casel.org) CASEL is a national organization dedicated to supporting students' success in school and in life. This website offers background information, news, tips, and tools.

National School Climate Center (www.schoolclimate.org) This organization is focused on building safer, more supportive school climates that will help fill students' social and emotional needs, as well as their academic goals.

Safe and Supportive Schools (safesupportiveschools.ed.gov) From the U.S. Department of Education, this website provides extensive resources on creating positive conditions for learning in K–12 schools.

Resources for Communities

Books

Benson, Peter L., *All Kids Are Our Kids: What Communities Must Do to Raise Caring and Responsible Children and Adolescents*, Second Edition (San Francisco: Jossey-Bass, 2006).

Green, Gary Paul, and Anna L. Haines, *Asset Building & Community Development*, Third Edition (Thousand Oaks, CA: Sage Publications, 2011).

Hechinger, Fred M., *Fateful Choices: Healthy Youth for the 21st Century* (New York: Hill and Wang, 1993).

Henderson, Nan (editor), *Resiliency in Action: Practical Ideas for Overcoming Risks and Building Strengths in Youth, Families, and Communities* (Ojai, CA: Resiliency in Action, 2007).

Hill, Sara L., *Afterschool Matters: Creative Programs That Connect Youth Development and Student Achievement* (Thousand Oaks, CA: Corwin Press, 2007).

Kretzmann, John P., and John McKnight, *Building Communities from the Inside Out* (Evanston, IL: Northwestern University Center for Urban Affairs and Policy Research, 1993).

Roehlkepartain, Eugene C., *Service-Learning in Community-Based Organizations: A Practical Guide to Starting and Sustaining High-Quality Programs* (Scotts Valley, CA: National Service-Learning Clearinghouse, 2009).

Websites

The Community Tool Box (ctb.ku.edu) This site from the University of Kansas presents an extensive collection of practical tools for all phases of community building.

Ready by 21 (www.readyby21.com) Ready by 21 is a national partnership that supports large-scale community mobilization initiatives. Its focus is on ensuring that all young people are prepared for college, work, and life by age 21.

Search Institute (www.search-institute.org) The Search Institute website provides extensive information on the Developmental Assets, as well as how to connect with other communities engaged in asset building.

Resources for Faith Communities

Books

Clark, Chap, *Hurt 2.0: Inside the World of Today's Teenagers* (Grand Rapids, MI: Baker Academic, 2011).

Dean, Kenda Creasy, and Ron Foster, *The Godbearing Life: The Art of Soul Tending for Youth Ministry* (Nashville: Upper Room, 2005).

DeVries, Mark, *Family-Based Youth Ministry,* Revised and Expanded Edition (Downers Grove, IL: InterVarsity Press, 2004).

Heflin, Houston, *Youth Pastor: The Theology and Practice of Youth Ministry* (Nashville: Abingdon Press, 2009).

Roehlkepartain, Jolene L., and Eugene C. Roehlkepartain, *Embracing Parents: How Your Congregation Can Strengthen Families* (Nashville: Abingdon, 2005).

Smith, Christian, and Melina Lundquist Denton, *Soul Searching: The Religious and Spiritual Lives of America's Teenagers* (New York: Oxford University Press, 2005).

Yaconelli, Mark, *Contemplative Youth Ministry: Practicing the Presence of Jesus* (Grand Rapids, MI: Zondervan/Youth Specialties, 2006).

Yust, Karen Marie, and Aostre N. Johnson, Sandy E. Sasso, and Eugene C. Roehlkepartain (editors), *Nurturing Child and Adolescent Spirituality: Perspectives from the World's Religious Traditions* (Lanham, MD: Rowman and Littlefield, 2006).

Websites

Faith Formation Learning Exchange (www.faithformationlearningexchange .net) This group provides research-based information on working with children, youth, families, and adults in Christian congregations.

Interfaith Youth Core (www.ifyc.org) IFYC brings together youth from different religious backgrounds to work together toward common goals based on shared values.

Jewish Education Service of North America (www.jesna.org) JESNA provides a variety of research, tools, and services to strengthen Jewish education among young people as well as adults. The website includes an extensive online resource center.

Resources for Young People

Books

Bingham, Mindy, Judy Edmondson, and Sandy Stryker, *Challenges: A Young Man's Journal for Self-Awareness and Personal Planning* (Santa Barbara, CA: Advocacy Press, 2005).

———*Choices: A Teen Woman's Journal for Self-Awareness and Personal Planning* (Santa Barbara, CA: Advocacy Press, 2006).

Canfield, Jack, and Kent Healey, *The Success Principles for Teens: How to Get from Where You Are to Where You Want to Be* (Deerfield Beach, FL: HCI, 2008).

Covey, Sean, *The 6 Most Important Decisions You'll Ever Make: A Guide for Teens* (New York: Fireside, 2006).

Jacobs, Rabbi Jill, *Where Justice Dwells: A Hands-On Guide to Doing Social Justice in Your Jewish Community* (Woodstock, CT: Jewish Lights Pub, 2011).

Kids' Random Acts of Kindness (Berkeley, CA: Conari Press, 1994).

Websites

What Kids Can Do (www.whatkidscando.org) What Kids Can Do is a group that promotes and supports partnerships between adults and young people working to make their communities better places. The website presents stories and perspectives from this work and from young people's lives.

Youthrive (www.youthrive.net) This nonprofit organization promotes collaboration between youth and adults to integrate peace-building activities into their lives, their communities, and the world.

Resources from Search Institute

Through its Healthy Communities • Healthy Youth initiative, Search Institute offers many practical resources for building assets in young people and creating healthy communities. Selected titles include:

- ▶ *150 Ways to Show Kids You Care* by Jolene L. Roehlkepartain

- ▶ *Ask Me Where I'm Going & Other Revealing Messages from Today's Teens* edited by Ruth Taswell

- ▶ *Assets: The Magazine of Ideas for Healthy Communities & Healthy Youth* (quarterly magazine)

- ▶ *The Asset Activist's Toolkit: Handouts and Practical Resources to Put Assets into Action* by Jolene L. Roehlkepartain

- ▶ *The Best of Building Assets Together: Favorite Group Activities That Help Youth Succeed* by Jolene L. Roehlkepartain

- ▶ *Building Assets in Congregations: A Practical Guide for Helping Youth Grow Up Healthy* by Eugene C. Roehlkepartain

- ▶ *Building Assets Reducing Risks: I-Time Curriculum* by Angela Jerabek, M.S.

- ▶ *Developmental Assets Profile* (DAP)

- ▶ *Empowering Youth: How to Encourage Young Leaders to Do Great Things* by Kelly Curtis

- *Engage Every Parent! Encouraging Families to Sign On, Show Up, and Make a Difference* by Nancy Tellett-Royce and Susan Wootten

- *Engage Every Student: Motivation Tools for Teachers and Parents* by Elizabeth Kirby, Ed.D., and Jill McDonald, M.Ed.

- *A Fragile Foundation: The State of Developmental Assets Among American Youth* by Peter L. Benson, Peter C. Scales, Eugene C. Roehlkepartain, and Nancy Leffert

- *Getting to Outcomes with Developmental Assets: Ten Steps to Measuring Success in Youth Programs and Communities* by Deborah Fisher, Pamela Imm, Matthew Chinman, and Abe Wandersman

- *Great Places to Learn: Creating Asset-Building Schools That Help Students Succeed* by Neal Starkman, Ph.D., Peter C. Scales, Ph.D., and Clay Roberts, M.S.

- *How Was* Your *Day at School? Improving Dialogue About Teacher Job Satisfaction* by Nathan Eklund, M.Ed.

- *Ideas for Parents* (CD)

- *Igniting Sparks* Out-of-School Kit

- *Instant Assets: 52 Short and Simple E-Mails for Sharing the Asset Message* by Search Institute Staff

- *Launching Your Teen into Adulthood: Parenting Through the Transition* by Patricia Hoolihan

- *Learn, Serve, Succeed: Tools and Techniques for Youth Service-Learning* by Kate McPherson

- *More Than Just a Place to Go: How Developmental Assets Can Strengthen Your Youth Program* by Yvonne Pearson, Kirstin Johnstad, and James Conway

- **MVParents.com** Visit www.mvparents.com for a wealth of free parenting resources by Search Institute

- *Parent, Teacher, Mentor, Friend: How Every Adult Can Change Kids' Lives* by Peter L. Benson

- *Parenting at the Speed of Teens: Positive Tips on Everyday Issues* by Renie Howard

- *Parenting Preteens with a Purpose: Navigating the Middle Years* by Kate Thomsen

- *Parenting with a Purpose: A Positive Approach for Raising Confident, Caring Youth* by Dean Feldmeyer and Eugene C. Roehlkepartain

- *Pass It On! Ready-to-Use Handouts for Asset Builders* by Jolene L. Roehlkepartain

- *Propellers: Quick Lessons to Launch Good Conversations* edited by Tenessa Gemelke

- *A Quick Start Guide to Building Assets in Your School: Moving from Incidental to Intentional* by Deborah Davis and Lisa Race

- *Safe Places to Learn: 21 Lessons to Help Students Promote a Caring School Climate* by Paul Sulley

- *Spark Student Motivation: 101 Easy Activities for Cooperative Learning* by Jolene L. Roehlkepartain

- *Speaking of Developmental Assets: Presentation Resources and Strategies* by Neal Starkman, Ph.D., and Clay Roberts, M.S.

- *Strong Staff, Strong Students: Professional Development in Schools and Youth Programs* by Angela Jerabek, M.S., and Nancy Tellett-Royce

- *Supporting Youth: How to Care, Communicate, and Connect in Meaningful Ways* by Nancy Tellett-Royce

- *Tapping the Potential: Discovering Congregations' Role in Building Assets in Youth* by Glenn A. Seefeldt and Eugene C. Roehlkepartain

- *Training Peer Helpers* by Barbara B.Varenhorst

- *Who, Me? Surprisingly Doable Ways You Can Make a Difference* edited by Tenessa Gemelke

To request a copy of Search Institute's current catalog, contact:

Search Institute
615 First Avenue NE, Suite 125
Minneapolis, MN 55413
Toll-free telephone: 1-800-888-7828
In Minneapolis/St. Paul: (612) 376-8955
email: si@search-institute.org
www.search-institute.org

Resources from Free Spirit Publishing

Founded in 1983, Free Spirit Publishing specializes in books and learning materials for kids, parents, and teachers. Many Free Spirit books address asset development. Selected titles include:

▶ The Adding Assets Series for Kids by Pamela Espeland and Elizabeth Verdick

▶ *Bullies Are a Pain in the Brain* written and illustrated by Trevor Romain

▶ *The Complete Guide to Service Learning: Proven, Practical Ways to Engage Students in Civic Responsibility, Academic Curriculum, & Social Action* by Cathryn Berger Kaye, M.A.

▶ *Doing Good Together: 101 Easy, Meaningful Service Projects for Families, Schools, and Communities* by Jenny Friedman, Ph.D., and Jolene L. Roehlkepartain

▶ *Everyday Leadership: Attitudes and Actions for Respect and Success* by Mariam G. MacGregor, M.S.

▶ *Fighting Invisible Tigers: Stress Management for Teens* by Earl Hipp

▶ *Going Blue: A Teen Guide to Saving Our Oceans, Lakes, Rivers, & Wetlands* by Cathryn Berger Kaye, M.A., and Philippe Cousteau

▶ *Growing Good Kids: 28 Activities to Enhance Self-Awareness, Compassion, and Leadership* by Deb Delisle and Jim Delisle, Ph.D. (eBook only)

▶ *Heart of a Warrior: 7 Ancient Secrets to a Great Life* by Jim Langlas

▶ *How to Do Homework Without Throwing Up* written and illustrated by Trevor Romain

▶ *I Like Being Me: Poems for Children About Feeling Special, Appreciating Others, and Getting Along* by Judy Lalli

▶ *A Kids' Guide to Helping Others Read & Succeed* by Cathryn Berger Kaye, M.A.

▶ *A Kids' Guide to Hunger & Homelessness* by Cathryn Berger Kaye, M.A.

▶ *The Kid's Guide to Service Projects: Over 500 Service Ideas for Young People Who Want to Make a Difference* by Barbara A. Lewis

- ▶ *The Kid's Guide to Social Action: How to Solve the Social Problems You Choose—and Turn Creative Thinking into Positive Action* by Barbara A. Lewis

- ▶ *The Kids' Guide to Working Out Conflicts* by Naomi Drew, M.A. (a Leader's Guide is available)

- ▶ *Kids with Courage: True Stories About Young People Making a Difference* by Barbara A. Lewis

- ▶ *Life Lists for Teens: Tips, Steps, Hints, and How-Tos for Growing Up, Getting Along, Learning, and Having Fun* by Pamela Espeland

- ▶ *Real Kids, Real Stories, Real Change: Courageous Actions Around the World* by Garth Sundem

- ▶ *School Power: Study Skill Strategies for Succeeding in School* by Jeanne Shay Schumm, Ph.D. (eBook only)

- ▶ *Stick Up for Yourself! Every Kid's Guide to Personal Power and Positive Self-Esteem* by Gershen Kaufman, Ph.D., Lev Raphael, Ph.D., and Pamela Espeland (a Teacher's Guide is available)

- ▶ *Talk with Teens About What Matters to Them: Ready-to-Use Discussions on Stress, Identity, Feelings, Relationships, Family, and the Future* by Jean Sunde Peterson, Ph.D.

- ▶ *What Do You Stand For? For Teens: A Guide to Building Character* by Barbara A. Lewis

- ▶ *What Teens Need to Succeed: Proven, Practical Ways to Shape Your Own Future* by Peter L. Benson, Ph.D., Judy Galbraith, M.A., and Pamela Espeland

To request a copy of the current catalog, write or call:

Free Spirit Publishing Inc.
217 Fifth Avenue North, Suite 200
Minneapolis, MN 55401-1299
Toll-free telephone: 1-800-735-7323
In Minneapolis/St. Paul: (612) 338-2068
email: help4kids@freespirit.com
www.freespirit.com

Index